Midwest Library Service
$39.94
P.O. 77921   ☝ P9-ARB-284
1-9-02

DISCARDED

Brooks - Cork Library
Shelton State
Community College

Brooks - Cork Library
Shelton State
Community College

Animal Experimentation
A Guide to the Issues

Animal Experimentation is an important new book for all those involved in the conduct, teaching, learning, regulation, support or critique of animal-based research. For perhaps the first time, all the major issues in the animal experimentation debate are introduced in one volume. This book covers the:

- history and ethics of experimentation
- moral status of animals and the obligations of researchers
- regulatory umbrella under which experiments are conducted in Europe, the USA and Australasia
- alternatives to animal research.

Although aimed at life-science students, its clarity of style will enable lay people and experts to read it with equal ease. Its balanced treatment covers the arguments that both support and oppose animal experimentation. Here, students and researchers will find a non-intimidating, readily understood introduction to the principal ethical arguments in the animal experimentation debate.

Dr Vaughan Monamy lectures in environmental science and environmental ethics at the Australian Catholic University, in Sydney. His research interests include wildlife ecology, with a particular emphasis on securing the long-term survival of Australia's native rodent populations, and human attitudes to animals.

DISCARDED

Vaughan Monamy

Animal Experimentation

A Guide to the Issues

CAMBRIDGE
UNIVERSITY PRESS

PUBLISHED BY THE PRESS SYNDICATE OF THE UNIVERSITY OF CAMBRIDGE
The Pitt Building, Trumpington Street, Cambridge, United Kingdom

CAMBRIDGE UNIVERSITY PRESS
The Edinburgh Building, Cambridge CB2 2RU, UK http://www.cup.cam.ac.uk
40 West 20th Street, New York, NY 10011-4211, USA http:/www.cup.org
10 Stamford Road, Oakleigh, Melbourne 3166, Australia
Ruiz de Alarcón 13, 28014 Madrid, Spain

© Cambridge University Press 2000

The book is in copyright. Subject to statutory exception
and to the provisions of relevant collective licensing agreements,
no reproduction of any part may take place without
the written permission of Cambridge University Press.

First published 2000

Transferred to digital printing 2001

Printed in Great Britain by Biddles Short Run Books, King's Lynn

Typeface Scala 10.5/15 pt.   System QuarkXPress WY21

A catalogue record for this book is available from the British Library

Library of Congress Cataloguing in Publication data
Monamy, Vaughan, 1958–
    Animal experimentation: a guide to the issues / Vaughan Monamy.
       p. cm.
    Includes bibliographical references and index.
    ISBN 0-521-66093-9 (hb) — ISBN 0-521-66786-0 (pb)
    1. Animal experimentation.   2. Laboratory animals.   I. Title.

HV4915 .M65 2000
179'.4—dc21   00-027642

ISBN 0 521 66093 9 hardback
ISBN 0 521 66786 0 paperback

We need another and a wiser and perhaps a more mystical concept of animals... We patronize them for their incompleteness, for their tragic fate of having taken form so far below ourselves. And therein we err, and greatly err. For the animal shall not be measured by man. In a world older and more complete than ours they move finished and complete, gifted with extensions of the senses we have lost or never attained, living by voices we shall never hear. They are not brethren, they are not underlings; they are other nations, caught with ourselves in the net of life and time, fellow prisoners of the splendour and travail of the earth.

Henry Beston (1928)

From *The Outermost House: a Year of Life on the Great Beach of Cape Cod* by Henry Beston. Copyright 1928, 1949, 1956 by Henry Beston. Copyright 1977 by Elizabeth C. Beston. Reprinted by permission of Henry Holt and Co., Inc.

Contents

Acknowledgements

The completion of any publication is rarely, if ever, successful without the able and willing assistance of many people. This book is no exception and it is a pleasure to thank the following people for the enthusiastic support they gave.

Parts of this book were originally published by the Australian and New Zealand Council for the Care of Animals in Research and Teaching as *Animal Experimentation: A Student Guide to Balancing the Issues* (1996: ANZCCART, PO Box 19 Glen Osmond, South Australia 5064). I wish to thank the Executive Officer, Dr Robert Baker, Professor David Mellor and board members of ANZCCART for their continuing support and encouragement.

Source material for *Animal Experimentation: A Guide to the Issues* was gathered principally from libraries at the Universities of Melbourne, Tasmania, New South Wales, Monash and La Trobe; the National Library of Australia; ANZCCART; and, especially, the State Library of Victoria (where spending day after day in the domed reading room provided inspiration).

I thank Jack Hider, Craig Steains and Stephen Daly for letting me share their home at Harper Street, when I didn't have one during the months of research in Melbourne. Their friendship, generosity and Craig's computer ensured that this book was well under way when it came time to move on.

Dr Michael Battaglia and Dr Libby Pinkard offered sustenance and support, and Dr Sally Bryant gave me unlimited access to her computer while I was staying in Hobart.

I thank Professor Michael Stoddart, whose worthwhile comments improved an early draft, and Professor Michael Degenhardt, who took the time to steer me through the shallows and reefs of moral philosophy.

I thank Anna Carew, Jennifer E. Taylor and, especially, Dr Catherine S. Williams who provided insightful comments and encouragement. Thank you, too, to Dr Tracey Sanderson and Dr Alan Crowden of Cambridge University Press for making the completion of this project positive, professional and prompt.

An early draft of this book barely survived the slings and arrows of an anonymous referee and I wish to express my sincerest thanks to my wife, Dr Miranda Gott, who convinced me that this work was worthwhile and that I should not expect to please all of the people all of the time. Miranda took time away from her own doctoral studies to balance destructive criticism with her own enthusiastic and constructive form. She is wholly responsible for me completing the task I had set myself and I dedicate this book to her.

The author is grateful for permission to reprint the following copyrighted material:

The frontispiece by Henry Beston, from *The Outermost House*. Copyright 1928, 1949, 1956 by Henry Beston. Copyright 1977 by Elizabeth C. Beston. Reprinted by permission of Henry Holt and Co., Inc.

Quotation on p. 1 by Miriam Rothschild, from *Animals and Man. The Romanes Lecture for 1984–85* (Oxford: Clarendon Press, 1986). Reprinted by permission of Miriam Rothschild.

Quotation on p. 25 by Major Charles Hume, from *Man and Beast* (London: Universities Federation for Animal Welfare, 1962). Reprinted by permission of UFAW.

Quotations on pp. 38–9 and pp. 49–50 by Albert Schweitzer from *Civilization and Ethics*, third edition (London: Adam and Charles Black, 1955); *Indian Thought and its Development* (London: Adam and Charles Black, 1936); and *My Life and Thought: an Autobiography* (London: Unwin Books, 1966). Reprinted by permission of Rhena Schweitzer Miller.

Quotations on pp. 40–1 by Nicholas Humphrey, from R. Rodd, Biology, Ethics and Animals (Oxford: Clarendon Press, 1990); and N.K. Humphrey, *Consciousness Regained: Chapters in the Development of Mind* (Oxford: Oxford University Press, 1983). Reprinted by permission of Oxford University Press.

Quotation on p. 47 by Tom Regan (1987), from 'The struggle for animal rights', in P.A.B. Clarke and A. Linzey (eds.), *Political Theory and Animal Rights* (London: Pluto Press, 1990). Reprinted by permission of Pluto Press.

Quotations on pp. 47–8 by Tom Regan, from *The Case for Animal Rights* (Berkeley, California: University of California Press, 1983). Reprinted by permission of University of California Press.

Quotations on pp. 53–4, p. 57 and p. 88 by Smith, J.A. and Boyd, K.M. (eds.), from *Lives in the Balance: the Ethics of Using Animals in Biomedical Research* (Oxford: Oxford University Press, 1991). Reprinted by permission of Oxford University Press.

Quotation on p. 71 by William Paton, from *Man and Mouse: Animals in Medical Research*, second edition (Oxford: Oxford University Press, 1993). Reprinted by permission of Oxford University Press.

I   Issues in animal experimentation

> Looking back at the first half of my life as a zoologist I am particularly
> impressed by one fact: none of my teachers, lecturers, or professors with
> whom I came into contact...none of the directors of laboratories where I
> worked, and none of my co-workers ever discussed with me, or each
> other in my presence, *the ethics of zoology*. No one ever suggested that
> one should respect the lives of animals in the laboratory or that they, and
> not the experiments, however fascinating and instructive, were worthy
> of greater consideration.
>
>   *Miriam Rothschild (1986, p. 50)*

AIMS

The purpose of this book is to introduce life science students to the major issues that constitute modern debate about animal experimentation. Many such students will complete tertiary studies and go on to become the new generation of scientists. Those in the medical and allied health professions may only be exposed to animal experimentation in their undergraduate years. Others, such as veterinarians, physiologists, biochemists, zoologists and agricultural scientists, may be actively involved in animal research at a postgraduate level and beyond. The welfare of animals in their care will be of major concern to their employers, the granting bodies that fund their scientific research, and to the public at large.

At some stage all such students will have to make a personal decision about the extent to which they are prepared to use research animals. Such decisions may influence potential career options. Most will be able to justify, to themselves and others, many forms of experimentation. Conversely, others will find that they are incapable of any intrusive procedure involving certain sentient animals. For some, sentience will not be an issue – they will be unable to experiment using *any* animals. I argue that decisions as serious as this ought to be taken only after informed discussion about major issues in animal experimentation.

These decisions will inevitably be made against a backdrop of differing societal and personal opinions about what is, and is not, appropriate treatment of animals. Adelma Hills (1994) reported ambivalence and inconsistencies in the attitudes of people towards the treatment of animals in general. In her survey, almost all respondents were comfortable with the idea of humanely killing animals for food. But what happens if you muddy the waters a little? People have vastly different opinions about the treatment of particular species. In western society, it is acceptable to kill lambs for food but it is unacceptable to kill dogs for the same purpose. What about wildlife? In Australia there is ongoing debate about whether kangaroos that are killed in pastoral areas when numbers become too high ought to be used for food. Again, opinions differ and rational arguments in favour of kangaroo culling for human consumption do not necessarily gel with the emotional responses people may have when considering the eating of that nation's symbol.

Similarities are evident in any discussion of animal experimentation. Surveys of attitudes to the use of animals for experimental and teaching purposes consistently report the majority of people in favour of such practices, where the procedures are important and suffering is minimised (e.g. Doyle Dane Bernbach, cited in National Research Council 1985; *Bulletin* magazine, 28 February 1984, cited in the Australian Government Senate Select Committee on Animal Welfare 1989; Media General 1985, cited in National Research Council 1985; Hills 1994). Most people, however, will never have to perform any animal experiments. Many of the readers of this book will, and it is my contention that it is these people who need to be most informed. You must be able to determine what you are, and are not, capable of doing, and to express these opinions clearly and openly.

This book, therefore, aims to introduce to its readers important issues which have arisen out of the animal experimentation debate that will assist them in making well-thought-out decisions. Not many students are fully conversant with the origins of modern animal experimentation practices, and fewer still with the intricacies of philosophical debate about the moral status of non-human animals. In western countries, animal experimentation is governed by legislation that aims to ensure that animals are used in ways in which suffering is minimised. It is

important to know how the day-to-day practice of animal experimentation is regulated. Are you aware of the increasing number of available
alternatives to using sentient animals in experiments? By the time you
have read this book, it is hoped that such information will assist you as
you explore your thoughts and feelings about the use of research animals. You, too, have a voice in any discussion of animal experimentation.

Debate over issues in animal experimentation has come a long way,
particularly since the 1970s. No longer does reasoned debate take the following form: opponent: 'All experimentation must cease!'; proponent:
'You're being totally sentimental; scientists know best!'. Instead (thank-
fully), contemporary discussions involve such issues as: what constitutes
an essential experiment? What is appropriate conduct when using animals in research? What alternatives to sentient animals are available? In
many countries (e.g. Australia, New Zealand and Canada), such debate is
conducted against a background of progressive legislation that ensures,
through a system of enforced self-regulation involving ethics committees, that all experimentation, from undergraduate rat dissections to
complex surgery on cats, dogs or wildlife, is reviewed and approved
before such procedures take place. Other countries (e.g. Britain) rely on
rigorous government regulation and a staff of inspectors rather than on
self-regulation. As this book goes to print, the British government is
instituting an ethical review process to complement the inspectorate system. Whatever the regulatory framework (see Chapter 5), its presence
also acts to ensure that most public concerns about the unrestricted conduct of experiments are allayed.

Nevertheless, whenever an emotive issue is under discussion, opinions will differ. For those who are vehemently opposed to the use of animals for scientific research, no experiment will ever be considered
essential; no conduct when using research animals will be deemed
appropriate. At the other end of the spectrum there still may be advocates
of scientific research free from any regulation. From this perspective, the
welfare of human beings will always outweigh the welfare of non-human
beings, and the quest for knowledge must never be hindered by what
may be interpreted as ignorance or sentimentalism.

Wherever you or I choose to stand along this continuum, we must
never lose sight of the fact that many of the medical benefits humanity

carries into the twenty-first century have arisen through the use of research animals. Dreaded diseases such as poliomyelitis were, less than 50 years ago, a scourge that ended many a young person's life. Survivors bore crippling limb deformities or were kept alive using artificial respirators. Because of experiments in which monkeys were integral, polio no longer poses the dire threat of only a few decades ago. When a vaccine is developed which reduces the risk of humans becoming infected with human immunodeficiency virus (HIV), it is certain that animals will have had a role to play in ensuring that such a treatment is safe for people to use.

So why is there a dilemma? Why do some students and researchers feel they are unable to conduct experiments involving certain animals? Why are scientists attacked, verbally and physically, for participating in research which may provide similar breakthroughs to that made in the containment of polio? What is it that some sections of society find so reprehensible in such scientific activity? The answers to all such questions have an ethical basis. Few in society would object to an increased quality of life, human or non-human, for reasons other than ethical ones. For some, it is simply that the price of such advances may be too high. Thinking opponents of animal experimentation argue that for every experimental procedure that involves research animals, the means must justify the end. Radical opponents of animal experimentation argue (sometimes violently) that the end can never justify the means.

For people not involved in animal experimentation in any direct sense (remember, everybody who buys commercial products that have been tested on animals, or who has taken antibiotics or many other forms of medication is involved, indirectly), it is a relatively simple thing to be generally in favour of, or opposed to, research that involves animals. Most people are not working in laboratories, however. If you are to be part of the next generation of scientists, you might be. Readers have to determine what they are, and are not, capable of doing with research animals in their care. After all, if you are unable to justify aspects of your work to yourself, you will have difficulty justifying them to others.

What you will learn in your chosen field is that science demands professional objectivity from its adherents – little, if any, room is available for subjectivity, sentimentality and value judgements. Yet you, as scientists, are only human. You may find yourselves in the position of having to justify certain activities conducted within your laboratories which, if conducted outside them, might be viewed as barbaric. A provocative example: why is it that a researcher can spend his or her weekend at home playing with a family pet and then, on Monday morning, return to the laboratory and test a potentially harmful chemical compound on stray or unwanted dogs? What is it about the donning of a white coat and the entering of the clinical atmosphere of a laboratory that can create an air of professional detachment? Opponents of animal experimentation may argue that such a scientist simply has ceased to feel. The scientists will argue that their work is of sufficient importance to the community at large to outweigh their feelings. Such scientists learn to manage the tension that arises between their professional objectivity and their personal feelings. For some readers, learning how to manage similar tensions will be an essential part of their education.

Contrary to what some opponents of animal experimentation may believe, it is both unfair and incorrect to state that western scientists currently conducting animal experiments are not fully conversant with their responsibilities. The overwhelming majority of practising scientists with whom I have been associated have a profound respect for the sacrifice made by their experimental subjects. They understand and work within their legal obligations and are in tune with the commonly voiced concerns of an increasingly well-informed general public. Modern society (rightly) insists that investigators increasingly pursue what are known as the 'three Rs' of modern research (Russell and Burch 1959). Namely:

- a *replacement* of animals in research, which follows on from an active development of alternatives;
- a *reduction* in the numbers of animals used in experiments;
- a *refinement* of laboratory and field techniques to reduce invasiveness and/or to increase the value of the results.

The 'three Rs' can be achieved in many ways. One tremendously important way is to alert science students to their future obligations as part of their curriculum. It should be an ideal of modern society that no university be able to graduate students from the biological or medical sciences who have not been educated formally in theories and practices that promote the humane care of animals used for scientific purposes. It is towards this goal that this book is directed.

DEFINITIONS

For clarity, it is necessary to define certain terms that will be used throughout. *Animal* is used in its broadest sense to encompass all animate life forms. Where necessary, I will differentiate between human and non-human animals. Much discussion about animal experimentation is concerned only with certain 'higher' animals. Instead of using 'higher' to describe those animals with which we most associate (i.e. vertebrates generally and certain mammals in particular), I will refer to their *sentience*. A *sentient* animal not only has an awareness of its surroundings but is capable of experiencing pain. Pain is a difficult concept to define and I deal with this in Chapter 6.

I use the term(s) *animal experiment(ation)* when discussing the use of live animals in research in the biological, psychological and medical technological sciences. The term also is appropriate to describe animal use in the production of biological extracts and the testing of consumer products, drugs and food. *Vivisection,* in the strictest sense, is the partial or complete dissection of live animals for research purposes. This is the definition that will be applied here. The word dates from a time when the majority of experiments involved dissection. *Anti-vivisection(ists)* is used to describe the stance of opposition (and its advocates) to this form of animal experimentation.

In many countries, research institutions now have committees that consider ethical aspects of research which involves sentient animals. They come under many names so in this book, for consistency, all are referred to as *Animal Experimentation Ethics Committees (AEECs).*

SCOPE

Currently, information on all aspects of animal welfare is available in many publications. Hundreds of documents have been written by moral philosophers, scientists and others advocating increased consideration for research animals. Many publications, too, are available that defend existing research procedures. In this book, I outline much of this extensive and specialised information for the readers for whom it is of the most value – the next generation of life scientists.

In the following chapters, readers will be introduced to the past, the present and the future of animal research:

- the origins of western vivisection are traced, and the parallel rise in opposition to such practices is discussed in context;
- some of the many advances in human and non-human welfare that have been made possible by experiments which have involved research animals are described;
- the principal moral objections to animal experimentation are introduced and readers are urged to find an ethical position with which they are most comfortable;
- the regulatory umbrellas under which experiments are conducted in western countries are discussed; and
- efforts made towards finding alternatives to animal experimentation are given their full due.

By the time they reach the end of this book, readers should be in a better position to consider their responses to the complexities inherent in any discussion of animal experimentation. References are provided for those who wish to enquire more extensively into particular areas of interest. Additionally, an appendix contains a list of recommended texts that offer further insight into aspects of the animal experimentation debate.

A history of animal experimentation

> Those who think that science is ethically neutral confuse the findings of
> science, which are, with the activity of science, which is not.
>
> *Jacob Bronowski (1956, pp. 63–4)*

THE ORIGINS OF VIVISECTION IN EUROPE

Early records of vivisection procedures provide sobering reading.
However, it is worthwhile to examine some of them in order to understand how public concern over animal experimentation arose. We need
also to consider the origins of western scientific practices and the prevailing societal attitudes towards them. Readers interested in a complete
history of animal experimentation and further insight into the historically important attitudes of humans towards non-humans are referred to
excellent discussions elsewhere (French 1975; Maehle and Tröhler 1987;
Rupke 1987; Ryder 1989).

Live animals, both human and non-human, appear to have been first
used in ancient times principally to satisfy anatomical curiosity. In the
third century BC, the Alexandrian physicians Herophilus and
Erisistratus are recorded as having examined functional differences
between sensory nerves, motor nerves and tendons (Singer 1957). Galen
of Pergamum (129–199 AD), a Greek physician working in Rome, cata-
logued these early experiments, as well as conducting his own. He
described, for the first time, the complexities of the cardiopulmonary
system, and speculated on brain and spinal cord function (Duckworth,
Lyons and Towers 1962). All such procedures were conducted without
anaesthetics (which were not discovered until the mid-nineteenth century) and it is interesting to note the expression of his feelings during
such experiments. When investigating the anatomy of the brain, Galen
preferred to vivisect pigs to '... avoid seeing the unpleasant expression of

the ape...' (Maehle and Tröhler 1987, p. 15). Galen (1956) left a legacy for future scientists. In *De Anatomicis Administrationibus* (On Anatomical Procedures), he detailed precise experimental methods and indicated which instruments would be best to perform many specific procedures.

Documentation of vivisection from the Dark Ages is scanty. It was not until Galen's records were re-discovered during the sixteenth century that there appears to have been any renewal of interest in anatomy and scientific methods. Such experiments often were conducted as public demonstrations. Belgian Andreas Vesalius (1514–64) and his students in Padua, Italy, illustrated public lectures on anatomy by using systematic non-human vivisection. An animal, usually a dog, would be cut open while still alive and the function of each organ would be speculated upon as it was located. It appears, from the records of these procedures, that the welfare of their experimental subjects was a low priority for these early vivisectionists. Maehle and Tröhler (1987) recorded that the experiments of one of Vesalius' pupils, Realdo Colombo (1516–59), involving pregnant dogs, were greatly admired by members of the Catholic clergy:

> Colombo pulled a foetus out of the dog's womb and, hurting the young in front of the bitch's eyes, he provoked the latter's furious barking. But as soon as he held the puppy to the bitch's mouth, the dog started licking it tenderly, being obviously more concerned about the pain of its offspring than about its own suffering. When something other than the puppy was held in front of it's mouth, the bitch snapped at it in a rage. The clergymen expressed their pleasure in observing this striking example of motherly love even in the 'brute creation' (cited in Maehle and Tröhler 1987, p. 18).

PREVAILING HUMANIST ATTITUDES TO NON-HUMAN ANIMALS

The Christian view

It may be difficult for readers to understand the apparent indifference to suffering exhibited in southern Europe at this time. What must be considered, however, is that the Christian church subscribed to the view that humans, blessed with the divine gift of reason, did not share a common lineage with other animals. Three hundred years earlier, St Thomas Aquinas (1225–74) had declared in his *Summa Theologiae* (1260) that humans were unique; all other animals were incapable of rationality because they possessed no mind. Only humans had a soul and the power to reason. Without a soul, non-human animals were merely objects, devoid of personality or rights. They existed only for human needs and were bereft of moral status (Linzey 1989). This is not to say that the Christian church supported a view that an absence of moral status meant that any form of cruelty was acceptable. The church recognised that the animals over which humans had been given dominion were a part of God's creation and, for that reason, were worthy of respect. Many animals, such as the dove, were symbolised as a part of Christian worship, and St Francis of Assisi was venerated because of his sympathetic attitudes towards animals. At the same time, however, Christian society did not see the infliction of pain on animals (or humans for that matter) as objectionable in itself, if it was an unintended consequence of some 'higher' purpose. However, the gratuitous infliction of pain was viewed as morally reprehensible cruelty. The inescapable suffering of animals during experimental procedures, such as that described above, was not seen in any way as cruel while it was conducted in the pursuit of greater knowledge.

Descartes and the influence of Cartesian thought

The seventeenth century saw an explosion of interest in scientific activity. British Lord Chancellor Francis Bacon (1561–1626) sustained the Christian anthropocentric (human-centred) view in his *De Augmentis Scientarium* (The Advancement of Learning, Bacon [1623] 1950). He asserted that much could be learned of the human body and its workings by vivisecting non-human animals and that such dissection obviated the need for the morally repugnant (but nonetheless fairly common) practice of human vivisection involving criminals.

Philosopher René Descartes (1595–1650) was to play an important role in early debate over vivisection. Christian-centred humanist attitudes, so prevalent throughout Europe, became exaggerated into a mechanistic philosophy following the publication of Descartes' *Discours de la Méthode* ([1637] 1984). Here, Descartes stated that it was possible to describe humans and other animals as complex machines: their bodies would obey known laws of mechanics. Descartes also believed, however, that the divine gift of the soul distinguished the human animal from all others. Only humans were conscious and capable of rational thought. Only humans were capable of acts of free will, and had true language. Only humans could declare *Cogito ergo sum* – 'I think therefore I am'. The reactions of non-human beings were dismissed as mere reflex, the response of automata (Rosenfield 1940). This concept of 'beast-machine' was critical to the way in which scientists viewed other animals. It provided a convenient ideology for early vivisectionists: how could animals suffer real pain if none had a soul? How could animals suffer real pain if none had real consciousness? In Descartes' writings was found a reason to discount the behavioural responses of animals to vivisection (which would be described as symptomatic of pain in humans) as the mere mechanical reactions of robots. Cries of pain in non-humans were now interpreted as the squeaking of un-oiled cogs. (Note, however, that John Cottingham, 1978, has argued for a reappraisal of the 'monstrous' Cartesian thesis. He believed that Descartes had been misinterpreted as denying *all* consciousness to non-human animals. A response to this argument is offered by Tom Regan, 1983, pp. 3–9.)

THE RISE OF MODERN BIOMEDICAL STUDIES

In a series of formative experiments conducted at the anatomy school in Padua in 1628, Briton William Harvey (1578–1657) demonstrated the circulation of blood using animals, extrapolated the discovery to humans and in so doing showed the value of vivisection not only for satisfying *anatomical* curiosity, but also for comparative *physiological* investigation (Harvey [1628] 1978). Questions, long pondered, about how we breathe, digest food and so on suddenly appeared to have physiological answers. As a result of Harvey's experiments, many other scientific investigators were eager to delve into the workings of the animal body. The rate of animal experimentation increased – an increase that was to continue beyond the seventeenth and into the eighteenth and nineteenth centuries.

Frenchman François Magendie (1783–1855) was among the first to determine that many bodily processes resulted from the co-functioning of several organs. This realisation set in train numerous experiments that involved manipulative procedures rather than just internal observations.

Although many of his experiments were 'hit-or-miss', Magendie is described as the founder of modern physiology (Ryder 1989).

Another landmark in physiology came with the publication of *Introduction à l'Etude de la Médicine Expérimentale* ([1865] 1957) by one of Magendie's students, Claude Bernard (1813–78). In this work, Bernard declared that a precise approach to experimentation must involve the study of one parameter while holding extraneous variables constant (this remains as a fundamental approach in modern science). In addition, he responded to a growing number of critics of vivisection by offering a powerful philosophical rationale for experimental medicine. Bernard ([1865] 1957) posed:

> Have we the right to make experiments on animals and vivisect them?...I think we have this right, wholly and absolutely. It would be strange indeed if we recognised man's right to make use of animals in every walk of life, for domestic service, for food, and then forbade him to make use of them for his own instruction in one of the sciences most useful to humanity. No hesitation is possible; the science of life can be established only through experiment, and we can save living beings from death only after sacrificing others. Experiments must be made either on man or on animals. Now I think that physicians already make too many dangerous experiments on man, before carefully studying them on animals. I do not admit that it is moral to try more or less dangerous or active remedies on patients in hospitals, without first experimenting with them on dogs; for I shall prove... that results obtained on animals may all be conclusive for man when we know how to experiment properly (Bernard [1865] 1957, pp. 102–3).

The work of physiologists such as Magendie and Bernard, coupled with the discovery of the anaesthetic properties of ether (by Crawford Long in 1842, and by William Morton in 1847), resulted in an adoption of technically sophisticated surgical procedures. Animal experimentation became routine in an increasing number of physiology laboratories throughout Europe. In Britain, the 1876 *Cruelty to Animals Act* (see Chapter 3) required meticulous registration of the numbers of research animals used in experiments each year. These records show that the number of procedures involving research animals increased from 311 in 1880 to over 95 000 in 1910.

The end of the nineteenth century saw vast improvements in aseptic surgical techniques and the development of bacteriology and immunology. Key medical discoveries, such as the discovery, in 1882, of the bacterium responsible for tuberculosis, and of a diphtheria antitoxin in 1894 (which rapidly reduced infant mortality from 40 per cent to 10 per cent in those afflicted), led to broad public acceptance of animal experimentation (Turner 1980).

More medical breakthroughs occurred at the beginning of the twentieth century, further emphasising the value of using animals in biomedical research. These included: the extraction of the first hormone (1902); a chemical treatment for syphilis (1909: French 1975); and the isolation, by Banting and Best (1920), of insulin, leading to the development of an effective treatment of diabetes mellitis (Bliss 1982). Such spectacular advances attracted enormous public acclaim and heralded the modern era of animal experimentation. In Britain, the numbers of animals used in experiments increased to exceed one million per year in 1943 and five million per year by the mid-1970s (French 1975). Numbers had declined to three million by 1991 (Australian and New Zealand Council for the Care of Animals in Research and Teaching 1993a), and were down to 2.7 million in 1997 (UK Home Office 1999, p. 9).

Increased government financial support led to the important improvements in preventative medicine and surgical techniques that today permit many to enjoy longer and enhanced lives. In 1989, the American Medical Association Council on Scientific Affairs published an impressive list of medical advances made possible through research using animals. It included studies of autoimmune deficiency syndrome (AIDS) and autoimmune diseases, anaesthesia, behaviour, cardiovascular disease, cholera, diabetes, gastrointestinal surgery, genetics, haemophilia, hepatitis, infant health, infection, malaria, muscular dystrophy, nutrition, ophthalmology, organ transplantation, Parkinson's disease, prevention of rabies, radiobiology, reproductive biology, shock, the skeletal system and treatment of spinal injuries, toxoplasmosis, yellow fever and virology. Such research has resulted in enormous gains in human knowledge, with subsequent benefits for human and non-human health.

This is an important point that deserves emphasis. We live in an unprecedented age in which life-threatening illnesses are kept at bay to an extraordinary degree. Having lived all of our lives at such a time, it is easy to forget that as recently as 50 years ago many diseases, such as polio and tuberculosis, were common killers in our society. In early Victorian Britain, life expectancy at birth was 42 years. Today, life expectancy at birth in most western nations exceeds 70 years (Paton 1993). One important reason for this increase in longevity (without detracting from, for example, the role of enhanced public health measures, clean water and occupational safety laws) is the benefits that have stemmed from animal experimentation.

Given such a track record, how could anyone condemn such practices? Surely increases in human health standards, as well as increased productivity of domestic livestock or increased general knowledge of wild animals through zoological and ecological investigations etc. outweigh any suffering involved in obtaining these advances?

This is at the heart of the matter. Some see that all experimentation is vital, ultimately beneficial and must be allowed to continue unchecked. At the other end of the spectrum are individuals who hold deep convictions that all animal experimentation is an abuse of other species for selfish human gain. If you choose a subset of humanity (say, the readers of this book) and quiz them on their personal attitudes, all will opt for a position somewhere along this continuum. Where you choose to stand will depend on many things, including career aspirations, vested interests, level of understanding of complex issues, personal moral views, religious beliefs, and levels of compassion for certain other animals. In the next chapter, readers are shown how objections to some animal experiments gained popular support, and why scientists increasingly had to defend particular experiments as essential before they were permitted to proceed.

3   Opposition to animal experimentation

How absurd, ... to say that beasts are machines, devoid of knowledge and feeling, which perform all their operations in the same manner, which learn nothing, which perfect nothing, etc! ... Barbarians seize this dog, which surpasses man so greatly in his capacity for friendship; they nail him to a table, and dissect him alive to show you the mesenteric veins. You discover in him the same organs of feeling that are in yourself. Answer me, machinist, has nature arranged all the springs of feeling in this animal in order that he should not feel? Has he nerves in order to be unmoved? Do not suppose such a pointless contradiction in nature.

Voltaire ([1764] 1962, pp. 112–13)

INTRODUCTION

Opposition to the use of animals for research purposes is not an entirely modern phenomenon. As the number of experiments had increased over time, so too had resistance to them. In western countries, rigid controls are now in force to prevent ill-considered exploitation of laboratory animals (see Chapter 5). These regulations had their origins in nineteenth-century Britain, where opposition to painful animal experiments culminated in far-reaching legislation. The 1876 *Cruelty to Animals Act* ensured for the first time that the welfare of laboratory animals was a legitimate consideration. It is of value to examine the reasons for the enabling of such legislation, and much of the ensuing discussion is derived from the British experience.

EARLY OPPOSITION

The first people to record their uneasiness with respect to vivisection were some professional physiologists. Only later did the general public become passionately involved. Professional opposition was based on a moral objection to perceived cruelty (remember, efficient anaesthesia was not available until the mid-nineteenth century). In addition, questions regarding the value of results gained from dying animals needed to be answered. Surely, '... the miserable torture of vivisection places the body in an unnatural state.' (O'Meara 1655, cited in Maehle and Tröhler 1987, p. 22).

Experimental physiologists Robert Boyle (1627–91), Robert Hooke (1635–1703) and Richard Lower (1631–91) exhibited genuine concern for the welfare of some of their experimental subjects. Boyle had gained general popularity during the mid-seventeenth century after he used his 'pneumatick engine' to demonstrate publicly the effects on kittens of being placed in a vacuum. Boyle spoke of excluding a kitten that had survived one air pump experiment from further trials because '...it was too severe to make him undergo the same measure again' (Shugg 1968a, p. 237). Hooke, after opening the thoracic cavity of a dog and observing the functioning of the animal's heart and lungs after the diaphragm had been cut away, kept the animal alive for over an hour by means of artificial respiration (a pipe inserted into its throat). In correspondence to Boyle, he confessed that he would be unable to repeat the procedure '... because it was cruel' (cited in Maehle and Tröhler 1987, p. 23). Richard Lower, also in correspondence to Boyle, drew attention to the tragedy of a donor dog's death during a blood transfusion experiment. At the same time, however, such men remained convinced that the costs in terms of the suffering of their experimental subjects were far outweighed by the potential, though unstated, benefits for humanity.

For the most part, early public opposition to vivisection was not based on a perception of cruelty. Rather, opposition was based on the argument that because of the fundamental differences (both anatomical and spiritual) believed to separate humans from other animals, little relevant benefit could be derived from experimentation on 'lesser' beings. Prevailing philosophical and religious views still regarded humans as completely different from other animals. Consequently, information gained by way of non-human vivisection could not legitimately be extrapolated to the human form.

By the eighteenth century, criticism of vivisection had become more widespread, but was still not a popular issue. Indignation was limited '... to scattered literati and the occasional humanitarian pamphleteer' (French 1975, p. 17). Perhaps for the first time, critics were questioning what was appropriate human behaviour towards non-humans. For example, in the last year of his life, poet Alexander Pope (1688–1744) became a committed anti-vivisectionist after witnessing the blood circulation experiments of Reverend Stephen Hales (1677–1761):

> ...he commits most of these barbarities with the thought of its being of use to man; but how do we know that we have a right to kill creatures that we are so little above as dogs, for our curiosity, or even for some use to us? (cited in French 1975, p. 16).

Pope was not alone. Samuel Johnson (1709–84) fiercely attacked vivisectionists through his weekly newspaper, *The Idler*:

> Among the inferior Professors of medical knowledge is a race of wretches, whose lives are only varied by varieties of cruelty...What is alleged in defense of these hateful practices everyone knows, but the truth is, that by knives, fire, and poison knowledge is not always sought and is very seldom attained. The experiments that have been tried are tried again...I know not that by living dissections any discovery has been made by which a single malady is more easily cured. And if knowledge of physiology has been somewhat increased, he surely buys knowledge dear, who learns the use of the lacteals at the expense of his humanity. It is time that universal resentment should arise against these horrid operations, which tend to harden the heart, extinguish those sensations which give man confidence in man, and make physicians more dreadful than gout or stone (cited in French 1975, pp. 16–17).

UTILITARIANISM AND THE RISE OF POPULAR CONCERN

A platform of opposition to vivisection was being constructed, consisting of three central planks. First, surely non-human animals were, at best, only questionable models of the human condition. If so, why were scientists so keen to use them? Second, eighteenth-century English essayists and poets were rejecting Descartes' beast-machine concept and were arguing that animals may well feel pain, and that this pain ought to be taken into consideration (Shugg 1968b). Third, and importantly, because anti-vivisectionists felt empathy with certain animals, compassionate people were looking for a philosophy that incorporated their concern for non-humans, arguing that animals ought to be afforded some form of moral status. Many sought to occupy this ethical dais and argument was passionate and persuasive. The predominant doctrines of Cartesian and Thomist (after St Thomas Aquinas) humanism were increasingly challenged by the new philosophy of *utilitarianism*. This creed professed that the only 'good' was pleasure and the only 'evil' was pain. To be a utilitarian meant that one should act to produce the greatest balance of pleasure over pain. The thoughts of philosopher Jeremy Bentham (1748–1832) played a central role in ensuing debate. He defined utility as:

> ... that property in any object, whereby it tends to produce benefit, advantage, pleasure, good, or happiness,... or... to prevent the happening of mischief, pain, evil, or unhappiness to the party whose interest is considered (Bentham [1789] 1970, pp. 11–12).

Did not a belief that animals were capable of feeling both pleasure and pain mean that they warranted similar consideration to humans? In *An Introduction to the Principles and Morals of Legislation* ([1789] 1970), Bentham emphasised that all humans were worthy of equal and humane consideration. As a footnote to this declaration he also suggested that a time may come when non-human beings would also be afforded similar consideration:

> The day *may* come when the rest of the animal creation may acquire those rights which never could have been withholden from them but by the hand of tyranny. The French have already discovered that the blackness of the skin is no reason why a human being should be abandoned without redress to the caprice of a tormentor. It may one day come to be recognised that the number of the legs, the villosity of the skin, or the termination of the *os sacrum* are reasons equally insufficient for abandoning a sensitive being to the same fate. What else is it that should trace the insuperable line? Is it the faculty of reason, or perhaps the faculty of discourse? But a full-grown horse or dog is beyond comparison a more rational, as well as a more conversable animal, than an infant of a day or a week or even a month old. But suppose they were otherwise, what would it avail? The question is not, Can they *reason?* nor Can they *talk?* but, Can they *suffer?* (Bentham [1789] 1970, p. 283: Bentham's italics).

Bentham was writing at a time when the French were beginning to oppose the capture and enslavement of Africans for labour in Europe and North America. It seemed only logical to him (but not to many of his contemporaries) that a similar ethical consideration ought to be extended beyond the human moral sphere to certain non-human animals. This was an issue that was to feature prominently in the development of anti-vivisection organisations in England in the 1800s.

An earlier, but less well-known, challenge to humanism came in 1776 when Humphry Primatt published his *Dissertation on the Duty of Mercy and the Sin of Cruelty to Brute Animals*. Here, Primatt extended the principle of justice beyond the sphere of humans, to include all animals:

> Now, if amongst men, the difference of their powers of the mind, of their complexion, stature, and accidents of fortune, do not give any one man a right to abuse or insult any other man on account of these differences; for the same reason, a man can have no natural right to abuse or torment a beast, merely because a beast has not the mental powers of a man (cited in Linzey 1989, pp. 32–3).

Primatt further insisted that:

> ... superiority of rank or station may give ability to communicate happiness ... but it can give no right to inflict unnecessary or unmerited pain (cited in Linzey 1989, p. 33).

The anthropocentric world view was being challenged by a more holistic notion that animals ought to be protected for their own sake. Whether an animal had a soul or not was no longer an issue – Primatt and Bentham had replaced it with a new criterion: *an animal's capacity to suffer*.

REVOLUTION DURING THE NINETEENTH CENTURY

At the beginning of the nineteenth century, animal anti-cruelty societies had been concerned almost exclusively with the abolition of the essentially working-class pursuits of cock fighting and dog fighting, as well as horse baiting and bull baiting. Membership of animal welfare societies was reserved for the middle and upper classes (who, apparently, saw nothing wrong with their own hunting sports: Rupke 1987). While institutionalised animal experimentation continued to be a greater-European phenomenon, few in Britain appeared concerned about its practice.

This attitude was to change following a scientific controversy that pitted the methods of an English anatomist, Sir Charles Bell (1774–1842), against those of the French physiologist François Magendie. Following public lectures in London in 1824, Magendie was accused of unnecessary cruelty in experimentation (Cranefield 1974). It is not certain whether the fact that one scientist was French and the other English created the controversy, but his actions provoked the following response from the editor of the London Medical Gazette in 1829:

> We recollect, some years ago, a violent clamour was raised against the practice of experimenting upon living animals...Certain lecturers were represented in the most odious light as unnecessarily torturing and sacrificing the lives of rabbits, frogs, dogs, and cats. The attention of the Parliament was called to the subject; the infliction of pains and penalties was threatened; and conviction, under a special statute, was, with difficulty, evaded. The appalling experiments of Magendie were the topic of the day; and...correspondence...excited a strong sensation (cited in French 1975, p. 20).

Physiology as a scientific discipline was responding to a growing insistence on consideration for the welfare of research animals. In England, a contemporary of François Magendie, neurologist and physiologist Marshall Hall (1790–1857), pioneered welfare issues from within science. As early as 1831, he proposed that physiological procedures be regulated in a way that took into consideration the suffering of animals (Paton 1993). Hall believed that five specific rules should be applied to all experiments. A researcher who adhered to these rules would be in a strong position to resist any public imputations of cruelty. As a first requirement, no experiment was to take place if the necessary information could be gained by observation alone. Second, only experiments that would result in the fulfilment of clearly defined and *attainable* aims ought to proceed. Third, unnecessary repetition of experiments must be avoided – particularly if reputable physiologists had been responsible for the original experiments. (Hall was later to call for the formation of a professional society of English physiologists with a journal to record all experiments and to keep members informed of current procedures: French 1975.) Fourth, all experiments must be conducted with a minimum of suffering. Finally, Hall proposed that all physiological experiments be witnessed by peers, further reducing the need for repetition.

Hall's far-reaching suggestions reflected an increasing societal abhorrence of animal cruelty, including painful vivisection. In Britain, the Society for the Prevention of Cruelty to Animals (SPCA) had been inaugurated in 1824 and its members committed themselves to the principles of kindness to animals, educating the general public about cruelty, and lobbying parliamentarians for the enactment of anti-cruelty legislation. Its objections to vivisection, however, were mild at first, and it maintained that some experiments were justifiable if conducted humanely. The SPCA received the patronage of Princess Victoria in 1835, and in 1840, as Queen Victoria, she gave permission for the society to use the 'Royal' prefix. Following the publication of evidence of the anaesthetic properties of ether in 1847, the RSPCA opposed all painful vivisection (French 1975). Throughout the nineteenth century, the RSPCA lobbied successfully for numerous changes to legislation. For example, the *Martins Act* (1822) was amended in 1835 to outlaw animal baiting; in 1854, dog-drawn carts were made illegal; and in 1869, game birds were accorded limited protection (Ryder 1989).

The 1870s, and the UK Cruelty to Animals Act (1876)

In June 1874, Queen Victoria expressed her concern over the treatment of animals used in experiments in correspondence accompanying a private donation to the RSPCA (Ryder 1989). This royal interest coincided with wide-scale English public opposition in the 1870s. The British Association for the Advancement of Science was under tremendous pressure to be accountable publicly for the behaviour of its members. The association had already published guidelines in 1871 that aimed to minimise suffering and discourage conducting experiments which were of dubious scientific merit (Phillips and Sechzer 1989):

• No procedure which could be performed with anaesthesia should be done without it.

- No painful experiment was justifiable if it were only being conducted to illustrate an already known fact.
- Whenever painful experiments were necessary, every effort ought to be made to ensure the success of the procedure, so that the experiment need not be repeated. For this reason, no such experiments should be performed by unqualified scientists with insufficient instruments or assistance, or in places not suited to the purpose.
- Operations should not be performed using living animals merely for the purpose of gaining new operative skills.

English society had been rocked to its foundations a few years earlier by the publication of Charles Darwin's *On the Origin of Species by Natural Selection* ([1859] 1964). Darwin had provoked furious debate with his theory that human and non-human beings had a common ancestor. In 1871, he addressed the specific issue of human origins in *The Descent of Man, and Selection in Relation to Sex* ([1871] 1981). He was convinced that his theory of natural selection must apply to all animals and that humans could not be excluded. In so thinking, he rejected the idea that humans were designed by God to stand apart from the rest of creation. Such an idea flew in the face of contemporary Christian theology, undermining arguments that all non-humans were a gift from God, to be used by humanity to their own ends. One such end was, of course, scientific curiosity – but, if we were related to the animals, argued opponents of vivisection, how could we use them in experiments perceived as cruel? (Darwin, himself, steadfastly supported the advancement of science through experimentation but was utterly opposed to any form of cruelty.) Science in general, and biological science in particular, was in the public spotlight as never before.

On 4 May 1875, a Bill aimed at regulating vivisection was presented in the House of Lords. Eight days later, a contrary Bill allowing for a regulation-free experimental environment was introduced into the House of Commons (Ryder 1989). Because of the contradictory nature of the two Bills and an increasing public clamour, British Prime Minister Benjamin Disraeli appointed a Royal Commission of Inquiry to investigate laboratory procedures involving animals. It reported back to parliament in the following year. Briefly, it found no specific instances of laboratory animal abuse in the UK but did recommend that, for the first time, animal experimentation be regulated (French 1978). The House of Commons set about preparing appropriate legislation to this end.

In response, a lobby group, the Victoria Street Society for the Protection of Animals from Vivisection, had been formed by Frances Power Cobbe (1822–1904) to argue for the legal restriction of vivisection. The Victoria Street Society (as it became known) attracted enormous support from many areas of English society. The most prominent members were clergymen, such as the Archbishops of Westminster and York, and the Bishops of Oxford and Carlisle. Other members came from the judiciary and parliament, including the Lord Chief Justice Coleridge and the Earl of Shaftsbury. The poets Alfred, Lord Tennyson and Robert Browning also were powerful lobbyists for the protection of laboratory animals.

Cobbe and others argued, among other things, that anaesthesia must be a compulsory component of all animal experiments involving surgery, and that animals should be euthanased without recovering from the anaesthetic (French 1975). The Victoria Street Society maintained that legislation was also required to prohibit the use of cats, dogs or horses for vivisection. A Bill was drafted along these lines, the *Cruelty to Animals Act*, and introduced to the House of Lords in May 1876 for debate. However, scientists were far from satisfied and, forming a lobby group of their own, argued for compromise in the area of anaesthesia. It was argued that, in some cases, the use of anaesthesia could adversely affect results; others argued for the necessity of recovery of experimental subjects in certain procedures. Many claimed the right to use any animal species for any purpose. Such lobbying proved successful and additional clauses were included in the draft legislation to permit such practices, where appropriate. Lobbying of individual parliamentarians by members of the Victoria Street Society and the RSPCA on one side, and members of the General Medical Council on the other, continued until August 1876, when the Bill received royal assent. In essence, the *Cruelty to Animals Act* (1876) required that any person wishing to perform experiments using live vertebrates must first be licensed, and all experiments involving cats, dogs, horses, mules and asses, or those conducted to illustrate lectures, be certified by the British Home Secretary.

The Victoria Street Society was disappointed with what they perceived as inadequate legislation and in 1878 changed their name (and aims) from '...the Protection of Animals from Vivisection' to the Victoria Street Society for the Abolition of Vivisection (French 1978). Eminent clergymen, such as the Archbishop of Westminster, Cardinal Manning (1808–92), argued strongly for this cause:

> ...at the present day we are under the tyranny of the word Science. I believe in science most profoundly, within its own limits; but it has its own limits, and, when the word science is applied to matter which is beyond those limits, I don't believe in it, and as I believe that vivisection is susceptible of such excessive abuse – such facile abuse – such clandestine abuse – all over the land, and by all manner of people, I shall do all I can to restrain it to the utmost of my power (Manning [1887] 1934, p. 11).

Abolition remained the goal of the Victoria Street Society until 1898, when internal divisions resulted in a more moderate line being taken by the re-named National Anti-Vivisection Society. Frances Cobbe resigned in protest and formed a new society, the rigidly abolitionist British Union for the Abolition of Vivisection. This society also had its champions, for example George Bernard Shaw:

> But I always regard a vivisector as a moral imbecile, and an intellectual imbecile. Consequently, I have a sort of benevolent feeling toward him, and I do not look upon him as an altogether grown-up and responsible person (Shaw 1912, p. 2).

Public campaigning towards the abolition of vivisection continued to be frequent and intensive. Anti-vivisection societies were considered fashionable by many of British society's élite. Consequently, the use of non-human animals for scientific purposes was never far from public scrutiny. Richard Ryder (1989) illustrated this depth of feeling. He described the erection, in 1906 in Battersea Park, London, of a bronze statue in tribute to a dog used in experiments by staff and students at University College, London. The International Anti-Vivisection Society, with the approval of the Battersea Borough Council, included a plaque that bore the following inscription:

> In memory of the brown Terrier Dog done to death in the laboratories of University College in February 1903 after having endured vivisection extending over more than two months and having been handed over from one vivisector to another till death came to his release. Also in memory of the 232 dogs vivisected in the same place during the year 1902. Men and women of England: How long shall these things be? (cited in Ryder 1989, p. 139).

In 1907, the statue was damaged by protesting medical students from University College, London. They insisted that the statue and inscription be removed. The council refused. The demonstrations that ensued were violent and uncontrolled. On 10 December 1907, about 100 medical students attempted to remove the memorial by force and were opposed throughout the afternoon and into the night by a large number of concerned citizens who wished to see the statue remain as and where it was. Mounted police were called in to keep the peace, arresting ten protesters in the process. In the weeks that followed, medical students were joined by veterinary students in pro-vivisection protest marches and, ultimately, a contingent of over 100 policemen had to be detailed to protect the statue from further attacks (Ryder 1989).

Two years later the statue disappeared and, to date, has never been found. A meeting called to protest its disappearance attracted several thousand demonstrators to Trafalgar Square, London. As a martyr, the brown dog had focused the attention of the public on what was considered unnecessary cruelty conducted under the auspices of science.

Continuous lobbying resulted in the Second Royal Commission of Vivisection (1906–12), but the public, buoyed by such spectacular medical advances as those described in Chapter 2, were less keen to condemn all experimentation. The influence of abolitionist societies declined and, after World War I, groups with more moderate goals rose to prominence. In 1926, the University of London Animal Welfare Society (later to become the Universities Federation for Animal Welfare, UFAW) was formed by Major Charles W. Hume (1886–1981). In 1962, Hume wrote that UFAW had been formed in part:

> ...to compensate the harm done to the cause of animal welfare by animal-lovers of the unbalanced kind, and to form an intelligently humane body of public opinion (Hume 1962, p. 202).

Notable among the achievements of this society has been the on-going publication, since 1947, of the *UFAW Handbook on the Care and Management of Laboratory Animals,* presently in its seventh edition (Poole 1999a, 1999b). Of equal importance was the commissioning of William Russell and Rex Burch to write *The Principles of Humane Experimental Technique* (1959), a guide which pioneered the notion of the 'three Rs', namely: to seek *replacements* for animal experiments whenever possible; a *reduction* in the number of animals used in each procedure; and the *refinement* of experiments to eliminate wasteful or unnecessary procedures. (The 'three Rs' are considered in detail in Chapter 6.)

BEYOND BRITAIN: OPPOSITION IN THE USA INTO THE TWENTIETH CENTURY

Medical research flourished throughout the western world in the twentieth century and perhaps nowhere more than in the USA. Several factors perhaps contributed to the USA's successful medical research efforts. First, there were greater opportunities to obtain research funding, notably from philanthropic organisations. Leading from this, it can be argued that American scientists were paid more and had higher professional status (and concomitant skills and training) compared with their European colleagues. Second, the USA had, for the most part, a rapid and sustained economic growth in the twentieth century, while Europeans were impeded by the social and economic effects of two world wars fought on their soil. Finally (and the subject of discussion here), perhaps it was the lack of concerted opposition to animal experimentation which delayed federal animal protection legislation until the 1960s and left scientists free to perform certain experiments that could not be conducted elsewhere.

A key reason for this delay in the enabling of legislation may well have stemmed from the amount of animal-based research that had been conducted in the USA in the 1800s. Far fewer animal experiments had been performed in the USA before the middle of the nineteenth century when compared to Britain, and American public interest in vivisection and its opposition was scant.

Despite this, welfarists such as Henry Bergh (1811–88), who had witnessed European animal experiments, tried to attract public support for the legislative control of vivisection in the USA. In 1866, Bergh founded the American Society for the Prevention of Cruelty to Animals (ASPCA), an organisation that was to argue unsuccessfully for the prohibition of vivisection in New York State in the 1870s. Following clashes in 1883 between welfarists and scientists in Boston and Philadelphia, some ASPCA members founded the abolitionist American Anti-Vivisection Society (AAVS) (Remfry 1987). Members and supporters of this organisation were successfully opposed by the National Academy of Sciences (NAS) and the American Medical Association (AMA), whose members argued for continued experimentation in an emerging era of major medical breakthroughs. Discoveries such as that of a diphtheria antitoxin in 1894 were embraced by an optimistic public excited by the promises of health and wealth that the new century was predicted to provide.

Arguably, the single event that was to determine the course of opposition to US medical research into the twentieth century took place in Washington DC in 1896. Although the cries of anti-vivisectionist societies had gone largely unheard by the American public, concern that medical scientists may have been using animals in painful procedures did not escape the attention of some humanist welfare groups. Influential organisations such the Women's Christian Temperance Union and the American Humane Association, together with the ASPCA, gained the support of a US senator in proposing legislation to Congress that aimed to restrict vivisection in the District of Columbia. Washington DC was a major centre of medical research, and scientists saw in the proposed legislation restrictions that would impact on the ways in which they could conduct research. Professional opposition to the proposed legislation was well organised through the AMA and NAS, providing medical testimony from American and British scientists promoting the benefits of animal-based research. In stark contrast to this professional approach, anti-vivisectionists only proffered old examples of vivisection derived from European practices. No attempt was made to illustrate their argument with contemporary American research that involved perceived cruelty, and the Bill was defeated in the House of Representatives (Rowan and Rollin 1983; Rowan 1984; Lederer 1987).

This result set the scene for how animal experimentation would be viewed (and opposed) for the next 50 years. The public showed little interest in listening to animal welfare organisations, and when any such organisation looked like garnering any popular support, pro-vivisection groups such as the AMA's Committee for the Protection of Medical Research would counter with lobbying and propaganda (Benison 1970). In the face of the enormous strides taken by medical research and with a quiescent animal welfare lobby, American humanists and social reformers tended to turn their attentions elsewhere. At the 1914 American Humane Society conference, a pro-research lobbyist was told that the society wished to 'leave vivisection alone' (Turner 1980, p. 118).

The use of animals in US biomedical research proliferated. Medical breakthroughs such as those listed in Chapter 2 buoyed the biomedical industry and encouraged the use of animals in other scientific pursuits. Modern experimental psychology began a rise to prominence. With it came an enormous increase in the number of behavioural experiments that used animals as models of human conditions. Russian physiologist Ivan Pavlov (1849–1936) had been the first researcher to describe conditioned physiological responses to specific environmental stimuli. His famous experiments on the salivation responses of dogs contributed to a fundamental shift in emphasis for the causes of behaviour from internal mechanisms to environmental cues. At the same time as Pavlov, Englishman Edward Thorndike (1874–1949) had studied the reactions of hungry cats. Experimental subjects had been put into a 'puzzle-box' with food placed outside. A specified response (pushing a lever to unlock the door) allowed the cat to escape and feed. Thorndike reported that, in early experiments, cats would obtain food through trial and error, but in later tests cats used learned behaviour (Poling et al. 1990).

In 1923, John Watson (1878–1958) introduced the works of Pavlov and Thorndike to the USA. He showed how such controlled experiments could be used to produce results that were both measurable and reproducible. Here was a rigorous scientific basis for psychology. Subsequently, experimental psychology extended the use of animals to studies that investigated memory, motivation, the interactions of mothers and their offspring, language and abnormal behaviour (Rowan 1984).

The Animal Welfare Act

With increasing numbers of scientists using increasing numbers of animals (cats and dogs in particular), there came a point when demand was predicted to outstrip supply. Anticipating this, a pro-research group, the National Society for Medical Research, lobbied some US state politicians to guarantee a supply of animals through pounds and shelters. First Minnesota, then Wisconsin, New York, South Dakota, Oklahoma, Massachusetts, Connecticut, Utah, Ohio and Iowa passed pound-animal 'seizure' laws in the 1940s that legitimised the procurement of unwanted animals for experimentation (Rowan 1984). Cats and dogs that strayed or were placed in animal shelters could be taken by researchers for vivisection. The increased use of cats and dogs in experiments resulted in the 'uneasy truce' between humane societies and the research lobby being broken (Rowan 1984, p. 51). Cats and dogs are probably two animal species with which people most empathise, and animal welfare groups were able to convince the American Humane Association that such laws had to be repealed and that an appeal to public sensibilities would win the day. A new organisation, the Animal Welfare Institute (AWI), was set up by Christine Stevens in 1952 to fight for the rights of the unwanted pets. These were animals, it was argued, that ought to have been provided with sanctuary when they were no longer wanted, but now they were being sent to their deaths in research institutions. Initially, the AWI lacked the lobbying potential of the pro-experimentation groups, but by progressively appealing to public sentiment, its members were able to gather the kind of popular support that successful politicians are quick to recognise. AWI members toured research institutions and reported instances of inadequate care (Stevens 1990), further alerting an increasingly concerned public that the time for research animal welfare legislation was approaching.

Two pivotal events that occurred in the early 1960s were to result in the proclamation of such a law, the Federal *Laboratory Animal Welfare Act* in 1966. Sixty years earlier in London, a brown terrier 'done to death' has focused public attention on the widespread use of dogs in British research (Ryder 1989). This time the concern of the US public was galvanised by the treatment of a Dalmatian called Pepper and an exposé by the populist *Life* magazine of the conditions in which starving dogs were kept by dog dealers in their pens (Mukerjee 1997). Pepper went missing and was thought by its owners to have been stolen and sold to a New York State dog dealer. Permission to visit the dealer's pens, first by the owners to confirm Pepper's identity and later by a congressman, was refused by the animal dealer and resulted in the politician (purportedly upset at the way he had been summarily dealt with by the dog dealer: Rowan 1984) introducing legislation that was to regulate the trade in dogs. The Dalmatian was never positively identified as Pepper and was used for experimentation prior to euthanasia and incineration. Once again, however, in attaining martyrdom in the eyes of the public, an individual dog advanced the cause of laboratory animal welfare in a way that countless thousands that had died before it had been unable to do. By eliciting a widespread emotional response, Pepper's plight had focused public and political attention on an aspect of animal experimentation that clearly warranted regulation.

A second event followed on from the Dalmatian's death. *Life* magazine (4 February 1966) published a photojournalistic article that exposed the shocking conditions under which dogs were kept by dealers prior to being sold for experiments. Public outrage ultimately resulted in federal legislation to license dealers and laboratories. In addition to licensing, the *Laboratory Animal Welfare Act* (1966) also required regular inspections of research facilities by the US Department of Agriculture (USDA) and accorded protection to cats, dogs, non-human primates and some rodents. The Act was amended in 1970 (as the *Animal Welfare Act*) to include any category of warm-blooded animals except livestock. However, in 1971, the USDA excluded mice, rats and birds from the Act.[1] The Act was further amended in 1976 to require the use of post-operative analgesia. Further amendments in 1985, 1989 and 1991 established institutional animal care and use committees (IACUCs), required appropriate veterinary care, imposed exercise requirements for dogs, stated that experiments must minimise pain and distress, and instigated guidelines for the psychological well-being of primates. Inspectors from USDA now ensure that such issues are addressed, and

[1]Despite long-term attempts by welfare organisations since 1971, rats, mice, birds, amphibians and reptiles, all of which are given legislative protection in Britain, Europe, Canada, Australia and New Zealand, remain outside the US *Animal Welfare* Act (see Chapter 5).

IACUC members now recognise these issues as significant IACUC-stated responsibilities.

As with the impetus for the enacting of the *Laboratory Animal Welfare Act* (1966), intense public attention, this time to the welfare of monkeys used in research, was to be the principal cause of the 1985 amendments. The 1960s and 1970s had been pivotal decades for the advancement of animal welfare in the US and elsewhere. One reason for this involved increasing public support for civil and environmental movements in general. Activists were fast learning that in order to gather popular support for a cause, the interest of the media was essential. In 1981, television channels broadcast pictures of the confiscation by police officers of 17 monkeys from a Maryland research facility. These animals (16 crab-eating macaques and one rhesus macaque) became known as the Silver Spring monkeys. They had been used in research relevant to the rehabilitation of human stroke victims, research that involved the deadening of all nerves in the macaque's forearms (deafferentation). The research was designed to see how the monkeys altered their behaviour in response to the deafferentation. The monkeys treated their forearms as being foreign to them and, at the time the police confiscated them, individual animals had chewed off their fingers. Additionally, it was apparent that the animals had been mistreated: some had untreated and infected wounds and the television crews were shown the filthy conditions in which the animals had been housed (Orlans 1993). Cruelty charges were brought against the Administrative Director of the research facility, Edward Taub, and the National Institute of Health ceased all relevant funding. The level of public exposure this event received through the media resulted in enormous public sympathy for the cause of animal welfare activists.

Increasingly, it was learned by welfare activists that turning acts of civil disobedience into theatre was much more likely to receive television coverage than passive protest or petition writing. This had direct consequences for the ways in which protests against animal experimentation were to evolve. In joining a moderate organisation, concerned citizens only had recourse to moderate campaigns in order to initiate change. In contrast, street demonstrations and sit-ins were seen as much more likely to accelerate the process of change. An extremist fringe believed they needed to go even further, and civil disobedience gave way to criminal trespass in research institutions and, in some circumstances, the theft of laboratory animals. One such act in 1984 resulted in the exposure of gross welfare abuses at the University of Pennsylvania, where baboons were being used in head-injury research (Orlans 1993). Subsequent media exposure of stolen videotapes showing the details of particular procedures and recording a total lack of regard for the welfare of individual baboons resulted in massive popular support for a strengthening of the *Animal Welfare Act* in 1985.

However, despite the 'ends-justify-the-means' approach of some activists, law breaking of this kind was never to be viewed favourably by the majority of the public, and illegal protests now are rarely, if ever, covered by electronic media. In a recent survey of animal rights demonstrators, criminal acts (including harassment of researchers and the liberation of laboratory animals) were rated as the least effective methods of advancing animal welfare. More effective methods were ranked as school education, company boycotts, legal protection, setting personal examples, marches and demonstrations (Galvin and Herzog 1998).

The 1970s and 1980s also saw increased interest in the welfare of animals among moral philosophers. Perhaps the most influential work to be published at that time, or since, was Australian philosopher Peter Singer's *Animal Liberation* (1975). This book provided a rallying cry for many opponents of animal experimentation by giving intellectual credence to what often had been criticised as sentimentality. Singer, reviving Bentham's utilitarianism, argued for the liberation of animals based on *equality of consideration* and their capacity to suffer:

> ...the fundamental common interest between humans and other animals remains the interest in not experiencing pain and suffering. The only acceptable limit to our moral concern is the point at which there is no awareness of pain or pleasure, and no preferences of any kind. That is why the principle of equal consideration of interests has implications for what we may do to rats, but not for what we may do to lettuces. Rats can feel pain, and pleasure. Lettuces can't (cited in Australian Government Senate Select Committee on Animal Welfare, 1989 p. 25).

Singer maintained that since laboratory animals were capable of feeling pain, their interests must be considered morally by humans. His principle of *equality of consideration* insists that all sentient animals be awarded the same level of consideration in any moral calculation. If the level of suffering in an experiment involving sentient animals is not outweighed by any increase in the quality of human life, it is morally indefensible to allow such an experiment to continue. However, an experiment may promise outstanding benefits that clearly outweigh the suffering of the experimental subjects. In such a case, a moral argument could be made for the experiment to proceed. Singer (1975) challenged scientists to argue that there was any difference between the moral status of human and non-human beings. If such a difference in moral status existed, how was it to be defined? If a difference could not be argued, how could scientists perform experiments on non-human animals that they would not be prepared to conduct using humans?

Although the majority of animal researchers did not subscribe to Singer's arguments, *Animal Liberation* (Singer 1975) was pivotal in rekindling debate (which had lain dormant for much of the century) over the relative worth (costs versus benefits) of animal experimentation.

Animal Liberation (Singer 1975) together with Richard Ryder's *Victims of Science* (1975) and, later, Bernard Rollin's *Animal Rights and Human Morality* (1981) were crucial publications in the resurgence of popular interest in the controversy that is animal welfare. These books were to focus public attention on clear instances where researchers were misusing animals in their care. The implication was that if research, such as that illustrated by Singer (1975) Ryder (1975) and Rollin (1981), was being conducted in certain institutions, was it not reasonable to assume that similar things were going on elsewhere?

Popular novelists, too, incorporated research-animal welfare into works of fiction to draw the attention of a broader readership to some of the poor experiments that had been conducted since the Second World War (see, for example, Richard Adams' *The Plague Dogs*, 1977). Scientists could no longer defend all experiments in the somewhat paternalistic ways of some of their predecessors. They were challenged to defend their practices in a philosophical arena and to demonstrate a morally relevant distinction between human and non-human beings that could justify the use of one but not the other in laboratory experiments. In Chapter 4, Singer's, and other, major philosophical arguments that have contributed to these changes are presented in more detail. Chapters 5 and 6 then illustrate the way in which modern science has responded to such challenges.

4   The moral status of animals

It is just not adequate for scientists to argue that there is a quantum difference between the moral status of humans and [other] animals if they are unable to give reasons for such a belief and defend their reasons in the arena of modern philosophical debate.

Andrew N. Rowan (1984, p. 260)

ON THE MORAL STATUS OF ANIMALS

Shaping the moral circle

It is doubtful that any issue in science has generated as much emotion as animal experimentation. In the previous chapter, readers were introduced to some of the historical reasons for the rise in opposition to vivisection. There had been three major components to criticism. First, how applicable to the human condition was scientific knowledge gained from experiments on non-humans? Early experiments, particularly prior to the discovery of anaesthetics, were crude and the results obtained were questionable. However, the use of increasingly sophisticated physiological techniques had led to a growing confidence in the reliability of experimental procedures. When this was coupled to a rigorous adherence to an evolving scientific method, the strength of this objection was reduced. Today, the dimensions and success of the biomedical industry attest to the acceptance and relevance of results gained from many species used as models of human conditions.

The second argument against vivisection had been based on the notion that, despite a prevailing Cartesian view among some experimenters that animals were incapable of feeling pain, cruel experiments were considered an affront to civilised (and predominantly) English sensibilities. The discovery of the anaesthetic properties of ether in the 1840s reduced support for this objection.

The third criticism of vivisection, endorsed by advocates of utilitarianism, that many animals were capable of suffering and therefore warranted *moral consideration*, was powerful. However, nineteenth-century anti-vivisectionists and twentieth-century animal welfarists were often viewed (and dismissed) as emotional animal lovers, unable to articulate their beliefs clearly in the face of authoritative science and medicine. It was not until the publication of central works by moral philosophers in the 1970s and 1980s that this situation was turned on its head. Philosophers such as Peter Singer (1975) challenged those who argued that there were fundamental differences in the moral status of human and non-human beings (and that these differences entitled them to exploit non-humans for the benefit of humanity) to show where the moral line between humans and other animals began and ended. In *Animal Liberation*, Singer (1975) highlighted incidences where animals were being exploited in industries as diverse as farm animal production, product testing and animal experimentation. He argued that, in the research arena, for example, the onus was on scientists to justify their experiments using, among other things, considered philosophical debate.

How does one measure the merits of a particular moral argument? Most scientists would admit to occupying a philosophical middle-ground between the protagonists who lobby for the abolition of all research involving animals and those supporters of a research arena free from any form of regulation. More intensive questioning, however, may reveal a reluctance to elaborate on a chosen moral stance. The moral implications for anyone involved in animal research are complex, and most scientists (indeed, most people) are unsure of the solidity of their position in such a philosophical discussion. This has been the cause of some concern. Rather than adopt a moral viewpoint regarding their own work, some experimenters may choose to assume a low profile while waiting for public anxieties to be assuaged by colleagues. It has been suggested that some scientists, perhaps, fear a too-critical self-inquiry because it might reveal a weakness in their particular philosophical point of view (Britt 1984).

Of equal concern is the attitude of some scientists that, as long as they remain within regulatory boundaries, their research is their own responsibility and there is no need to be accountable publicly. For example, in a pamphlet published by the British Physiological Society's Education Sub-Committee (1983), physiological experiments involving animals were defended to young scientists. It was argued that physiologists should be guided by their consciences as to what was acceptable experimental technique, but that the goal of good science ought to be uppermost in their minds: '...animal experimentation poses ethical problems, because we are ourselves animals and we have, or possibly we imagine we have, empathy with other animals'. Arguments relating to a reduction in the numbers of animals used in experiments were dismissed: 'On moral pressures to use less [sic] animals, you and your colleagues in the scientific community are the only judges of the numbers needed. It is your reputation; you must stand firm' (cited in Langley 1989, p. 208).

Both the 'head-in-the-sand' stance and the 'rule-book scientist' point of view are, fortunately, becoming the exception rather than the rule as more scientists move forward to grapple with the intricacies of contemporary ethical debate.

The shaping of the moral line between human and non-human beings continues. Individual attitudes towards animals are diverse and shifting, and societal interchanges between humans and non-humans are complex. Today, every student and researcher involved in animal experimentation should consider a number of ethical questions. One such question will suffice to illustrate how difficult each is to answer. Many non-human animals are used in experiments because they are so like us – this makes them good models of human conditions in biomedicine. But if these animals are so like us, why do we treat them so differently? To do so, Peter Singer (1978; 1990, pp. 27–91) argued, is to disregard their *interests*, while for Tom Regan (1981; 1982, pp. 363–94), it is in contravention of their *rights*.

This chapter examines Singer's and Regan's ethical arguments of animal 'interests' and animal 'rights' in detail. Their influence in modern debate is examined and the relative strengths and weaknesses of their arguments are highlighted. Additionally, further ethical viewpoints relevant to any discussion of the moral status of animals are outlined. First, humanism is described. Second, some have argued for an ethic not based exclusively on philosophical reason, but which also incorporates the emotionally derived concepts of empathy and compassion. Such an ethic closely reflects the beliefs of Albert Schweitzer and the universality of his ideal of 'reverence for life' (Schweitzer 1936).

Despite genuine attempts by philosophers to achieve agreement about the width of the moral gulf between humans and other animals, no single ethical thesis has been universally accepted. This has important implications for debate about animal experimentation, where agreement would be invaluable. In the absence of such a consensus, some have proposed a form of practical moral stewardship by researchers for animals in their care. This also will be detailed.

As you will see, each ethical stance has its flaws, each has its critics. Nevertheless, each will serve to illustrate the breadth of the different opinions held in scientific and philosophical circles. Note, however, that while the points of view which follow are important in stimulating discussion, they must not be seen as the *only* ideas on the moral status of animals (interested readers are referred to Stephen Clark's excellent coverage of further ideas in *The Moral Status of Animals*, 1984).

Expanding the moral circle

What are ethics? What is morality? When we discuss ethics and morality we refer to appropriate human conduct: what we ought to do, and why, in certain circumstances. *Ethic* is derived from the Greek *ethos* meaning custom, people or system: *ethos* refers to the predominant community spirit. *Morality* is the distinction between right and wrong within that community spirit.

Historically in western communities, socially responsible human conduct has meant concern for others besides oneself, and with the welfare of *human* society as a whole. Some philosophers and moral thinkers have argued for more expansive definitions. For example, early in the twentieth century, Albert Schweitzer examined prevailing anthropocentric ethical views (based in part on the thoughts of philosopher Immanuel Kant) and found them wanting. Schweitzer insisted that for the truly ethical person, *all* life (not just human life) was sacred and, therefore, worthy of moral consideration:

> [Ethics] must widen the circle from the narrowest limits of the family first to include the clan, then the tribe, then the nation and finally all mankind. But even when it has established the relationship between

man and every other man it cannot stop. By reason of the quite universal idea ... of participation in a common nature, it is compelled to declare the unity of mankind with all created beings (Schweitzer 1955, p. 261).

Others, including Aldo Leopold in *A Sand County Almanac* (1949), went further and argued for a comprehensive *environmental* ethic. Such an ethic (a 'land ethic') would incorporate not only life-forms (human and non-human), but entire ecosystems, including the physical environment, the interactions between organisms, and between organisms and their non-living environment.

The land ethic simply enlarges the boundaries of the [ethical] community to include soils, waters, plants and animals, or collectively, the land (Leopold 1949, p. 219).

Enlarging the ethical community beyond the human sphere requires a total reconsideration of which features are morally relevant. In *The Rights of Nature*, Roderick Nash (1990, p. 4), recognised as '...one of the most extraordinary developments in recent intellectual history...' the development of the relationship between humans and nature into an ethical one. He described, as Schweitzer had previously, how modern western ethics evolved from a pre-ethical past, where first the sphere of consideration was restricted only to the self. This had then expanded progressively to include kin, tribe and neighbours. Western ethical ideals over recent centuries have also urged a moral consideration of one's nation, one's race and finally all humanity. Nash predicted that the logical extension of ethical concern would next include all animals, then plants, all life, ecosystems, the planet and, finally, the universe.

It is one thing to make such a prediction, another to argue that it is defensible, desirable or justifiable. What we can see, though, is that before you and I can make a decision about an appropriate ethic of animal experimentation, we are confronted by differences of opinions about what sorts of ethics we could adopt as individuals. Kant was anthropocentric, i.e. human beings have a special value; Schweitzer argued that all life had moral relevance; for Leopold it was all life and ecosystems; and for Nash, perhaps, the entire universe. Whether we believe that appropriate human conduct involves only humans, or humans *and* certain mammals, or all animals *and* plants but not rocks, is something on which consensus is yet to be reached.

MORAL ARGUMENTS BASED ON REASON

The re-defining of a society's ethics and morals has generally coincided with historical turning-points, such as emancipation from slavery. The twentieth century witnessed a continuation of this trend. The 1960s and 1970s were crucial decades for those committed to the ideal of freedom from discrimination for women and non-white races. A quantum extension of ethics was proposed when Peter Singer asserted in *Animal Liberation* (1975) that moral consideration must transcend the species boundary to include all sentient animals. Since then, contributions by philosophers to discussion of the moral status of animals and the consequences for their use for scientific purposes have been far-reaching. Reasoned intellectual debate has increasingly replaced the violent and illegal demonstrations thought necessary by some anti-vivisectionists, and has led to a reduction in insularity on the part of many researchers. Few scientists would now regard the criticisms of moderate welfarists as merely the rantings of ill-informed sentimentalists.

In order to clarify the moral issues which have been proposed as relevant to a discussion of animal experimentation, it is helpful to consider first a number of rationally based ethical stances.

Humanist views

Today, few thinkers are willing to advocate the Cartesian view of humanism, that is, that all non-human animals are insentient and, therefore, incapable of feeling pain. However, some, such as British psychologist Nicholas Humphrey, have offered their opinion that non-human animals are without self-consciousness:

> ...Descartes was as nearly right as makes no matter. If we walk down an English county lane, we walk by ourselves. Trees, birds, bees, the rabbit darting down its hole, the cow heavy with milk waiting at the farmer's gate are all as without insight into their condition as the dummies on show at Madame Tussaud's (cited in Rodd 1990, p. 42).

... and possibly without any form of consciousness:

> ...indeed we cannot be sure that animals consciously feel anything at all. Appearances notwithstanding, it is logically possible that animals are (as Descartes believed) merely unconscious automata (Humphrey 1983, p. 42).

Such views are not widely held. Important studies of self-recognition using chimpanzees and mirrors have shown that some animals (other than humans) are capable of recognising themselves. Gordon Gallup (cited in Denton 1993, pp. 55–65) anaesthetised captive chimpanzees and, while they were unconscious, painted red markers above one eyebrow and the top of their opposite ear. The dye was odourless and positioned so that the chimps could not see that they had been marked. When each chimp regained consciousness, a mirror was introduced into its cage (one chimp, one mirror per cage; every individual had been exposed to mirrors prior to the experiment) and a careful score of the number of times each chimp touched the dye marker was kept. Gallup found that the number of times the area around the mark was touched rose 25-fold when compared with random touching prior to the introduction of the mirror. If a chimpanzee, on seeing its reflection, interpreted that reflection as another individual rather than itself, would not the chimp touch the mirror rather than it's own head? As Derek Denton (1993, p. 60) concluded:

> ...you cannot examine otherwise-invisible portions of your body with the aid of a reflection unless you know who you are – that is, the animal is aware of itself.

If one is to argue that humans differ from non-humans because of our level of consciousness or self-consciousness, we must see that the difference is one only of degree, not of kind. If some primates other than ourselves are capable of some form of consciousness, what of others? If we are arguing over degrees of consciousness, has not the demarcation between humans and non-humans become just a little fuzzy?

A humanist might suggest other criteria which make humans worthy of ethical consideration, such as our advanced communication skills, or our (sometime) propensity to altruism, but critics will always counter all such reasons with examples from the non-human animal kingdom. Carl Sagan and Ann Druyan (1992) are particularly adept at this.

Immanuel Kant (1724–1804) believed that appropriate human conduct (morality) did not extend beyond the human sphere because only humans were an end in themselves. All other animals were seen as a means to an end. He argued that overt cruelty to animals was to be avoided, not because humans had any form of duty to them, but rather because humans had indirect duties to humanity. Cruelty could never be defended, because: '...he who is cruel to animals becomes hard also in his dealings with men' (cited in Infield 1963, p. 239).

This way of thinking perhaps had an earlier precedent in William Shakespeare's *Cymbeline*:

> Queen (addresses Cornelius):   I will try the forces of these thy
>   [poisons] on such creatures as we
>   count not worth the hanging, but
>   none human ...
>
> Cornelius: Your highness, shall from this
>   practice but make hard your
>   heart?
>
>   (Shakespeare 1982, p. 970)

Traditional Kantian humanism acknowledges that sentient animals are capable of suffering, but argues that all non-human animals lack the critical quality of moral autonomy or personhood which makes humans so unique. Without moral autonomy there can be no understanding of duty, so, other animals, while worthy of our moral concern, cannot be afforded any moral status in their own right.

The problem with applying Kantian humanist theory to the practical day-to-day conduct of animal experiments does not involve the breadth of the moral divide between humans and non-humans. Rather, it is its failure to make a theoretical distinction between animal species *beyond* the human sphere. Consequently, this strictly humanist viewpoint can morally justify the use of a chimpanzee in an experiment where a laboratory rat would suffice, because neither species has moral autonomy.

In all countries which have laboratory animal laws, however, the legislation and day-to-day regulation of animal experiments do not reflect this: both make hierarchical distinctions between non-human species (see further discussion in this chapter and in Chapter 5).

Singer and animal 'interests'

Around the same time as Kant, Jeremy Bentham ([1789] 1970, p. 283) alluded to an ethical expansion beyond the human domain when he asked of other animals: 'The question is not Can they *reason?* nor Can they *talk?*, but Can they *suffer?*' Peter Singer (1975) revived Bentham's utilitarian claim that equal consideration must be given to all beings that were capable of suffering, *based upon that capacity to suffer*. He adopted an ethical stance which has proved to be pivotal. He argued that moral judgements must be made based on equal interests and, in the same way as we should never be influenced by race or sex, we should never be influenced by species:

> If a being suffers, there can be no moral justification for refusing to take that suffering into consideration. No matter what the nature of the being, the principle of equality requires that its suffering be counted equally with the like suffering – in so far as rough comparisons can be made – of any other being (Singer 1993, p. 57).

In other words, before taking any action which may involve distress, a utilitarian must perform a moral calculation. If an action (say, an animal experiment) leads to a net increase in the amount of 'good' for sentient (especially human) life, then that action is justified. If, however, a particular action causes more 'evil' for more sentient creatures than it produces 'good' for others, then that action is not justified.

Singer (1990) does not argue that all sentient species are of equal worth. Rather, as a *preference utilitarian*, he supports the idea that human beings, because of a combination of capacities which include self-awareness, acute intelligence, complex language and the ability to plan for the future, are entitled to specific preference for continued existence. Nevertheless, it is not possible to argue that smarter (or stronger) is better and therefore the use of less intelligent (or weaker) animals is justified. To adopt such a 'might makes right' attitude essentially invalidates all morality (Rowan and Rollin 1983). Nor does Singer (1990, p. 85) argue that his moral calculation will necessarily lead to the prohibition of all animal experimentation, because:

> ...in extreme circumstances, absolutist answers always break down... if a single experiment could cure a disease like leukemia, that experiment would be justifiable.

But Singer (1990, p. 85) does assert:

> ...in actual life the benefits are always more remote and more often than not they are non-existent...an experiment cannot be justifiable unless the experiment is so important that the use of a brain-damaged human would also be justifiable.

Here, Singer is not advocating the use of mentally retarded people in experiments (although this accusation has been levelled at him recently: (Singer 1993, pp. 337–59). His point is that it is morally indefensible to countenance experimentation using other animals, rather than experimentation using humans with similar abilities to comprehend their situation, if the decision to use non-human animals is based on the subject of species difference. Singer (1993) argues that such a view is *speciesism* and is as unjustifiable in a moral community as racism or sexism.

Regan and animal 'rights'

A third moral view, supported most strongly by Tom Regan (1981, 1982, 1983, 1985, 1990), involves animal *rights*. Regan has proposed that the 'inherent value' of an individual (of any species) must be measured by its experience of the importance of its own life to itself. 'Inherent value' is the value of conscious individuals regardless of their usefulness to others, and independent of their 'goodness'. Equal rights for such individuals protect their 'inherent value' and give it (and them) moral status.

Regan has argued that any dealings which humans have with non-humans involve some exploitation of their rights. When it comes to animal experimentation, his views are unequivocal:

> ...the rights view is categorically abolitionist...This is just as true when [animals] are used in trivial, duplicative, unnecessary or unwise research as it is when they are used in studies that hold out real promise of human benefits...The best we can do when it comes to using animals in science is – not to use them (Regan 1985, p. 24).

Animal interests and animal rights: strengths

Of the moral views summarised above, the latter two have had the most impact on the way in which animal experiments are now conducted. In 1978, Singer predicted that the earlier publication of works by himself

(Singer 1975), Regan and Singer (1976) and Richard Ryder (1975) would result in the elevation of debate beyond the unproductive arena of name-calling and ill-founded accusation, to the productive realm of reasoned philosophical debate (Singer 1978). The ideas put forward by Singer and Regan have provided a sensible departure point for debate over the moral issues essential in any rational discussion of animal experimentation. It has not been productive to counter logical philosophical arguments with rhetoric or emotional responses. The evolution of such arguments has led to meaningful dialogue between those who conduct experiments using animals and those who are concerned with animal welfare. Since Singer (1978) made his prediction, professional and popular support has indeed brought about a fundamental shift in the way in which non-human beings are perceived and has resulted in immeasurable improvements in the welfare of research animals.

An example of this support for the expansion of ethics beyond the human sphere was reported by Nicholas Wade (1978) in the *Science* journal. An application was lodged by a pharmaceutical company with the US Fisheries and Wildlife Service to import chimpanzees (an endangered species) into the USA from Sierra Leone in the mid-1970s. It was intended that these chimpanzees would be used to test a potential vaccine against the virus which causes human hepatitis B. It was known that the capture of juvenile chimpanzees often involved the shooting of their mothers by uncaring trappers, but at that time about 1500 people were dying each year from hepatitis B in the USA. Wade (1978, p. 1030) concluded:

> The world has a growing population of [then] four billion people and a dwindling population of some 50,000 chimpanzees. Since the vaccine seems unusually innocuous, and since the disease is only rarely fatal, it would perhaps be more just if the larger population could find some way of solving its problem that was not to the detriment of the smaller.

Many people, including members of an order of monks, volunteered to have trials conducted on them rather than on chimps. The application to use chimpanzees in this research was opposed by, among others, the International Primate Protection League and was rejected, principally because of an ethical stance that urged that threatened species should not be used in safety testing (Rolston 1988).

Animal interests and animal rights: weaknesses

The views of both Singer and Regan have not been immune to criticism, notably for polarising debate. Additionally, Singer's style of preference utilitarianism has been criticised for its lack of consistency. Moral calculations become tortuous and impractical when all factors are taken into consideration. Just how do you quantify an amount of pleasure or pain? James Battye (1994) considered the application of utilitarianism to the Roman Colosseum, where Christians were being used for sport. A 'do-gooder' complains to the Emperor that such practice is evil: 'Evil?' says the Emperor, 'That's easily fixed: we'll sell more tickets' (Battye 1994, p. 5). The point Battye is emphasising is that an act considered 'evil' can be negated so long as you can increase the 'good' that it also brings about.

Tom Regan (1982, p. 46) also has argued that: '... the animal industry is big business'. What he meant was, biomedicine employs hundreds of thousands of people who, in turn, have hundreds of thousands of dependants. A preference utilitarian (such as Singer) must take into consideration the interests of all such people if one is to advocate the reduction or closure of the industries which use research animals. Under Singer's terms, aren't such people's interests (in being employed and able, therefore, to support their families) of more importance than those of the research animals?

Others are also critical of utilitarianism, as it applies beyond the human sphere. For some, it simply does not go far enough – there is more to life, any life, than just pleasure and pain. Eminent Australian scientist and philosopher Charles Birch (1993, pp. 86–96) posed an interesting question: if all animals used for human purposes were to be constantly anaesthetised for all of their lives, thereby eliminating the pleasure/pain argument, would such a procedure be morally defensible?

Regan's unshakeable beliefs in moral rights based on unquantifiable 'inherent value' have also been challenged on numerous grounds. Some claim, for example, that rights can be attributed only to individuals who can claim them, and that they can only apply in circumstances where that individual understands the notions of rights (i.e. only some humans:

Smith and Boyd 1991). Regan has countered by pointing out that such a viewpoint would withhold rights from infants, the mentally retarded and the senile. Do not all humans have the same rights?:

> Animals, it is true, lack many of the abilities humans possess. They can't read, do higher mathematics, build a bookcase or make *baba ghanoush*. Neither can many human beings, however, and yet we don't (and shouldn't) say that they (these humans) therefore have less inherent value, less of a right to be treated with respect, than do others (Regan 1990, pp. 184–5; Regan's italics).

Others have attacked the absence of a clear distinction between 'moral' and 'legal' rights for individual animals of all species. Not all species have moral rights; only one has legal rights (see Remfry 1987, pp. 12–13, for a summary of this argument).

Further criticism deals with Regan's criterion for a claim to inherent value (and hence membership within a moral circle): 'Inherent value belongs equally to those who are the experiencing subjects-of-a-life' (Regan 1990, p. 186). To satisfy this criterion, an animal must be, among other things, conscious, have the capacities necessary to conceive the future, and to act deliberately. According to Regan, the only beings which satisfy this criterion are '... mentally normal *mammals* of a year or more [in age]' (Regan 1983, p. 78: my italics). J. Baird Callicott (1989, pp. 39–47) was especially critical of this feature of the 'animal rights' thesis. (Why not 'mammal rights'?) In particular, Callicott (1989, pp. 40–1) criticised Regan's ecological naïveté. He referred to the following two passages from Regan's *The Case for Animal Rights* (1983) as evidence of the general inapplicability of the rights concept to biological conservation:

> Species are not individuals, and the rights view does not recognize the moral rights of species to anything, including survival (Regan 1983, p. 359).

and:

> That an individual animal is among the last remaining members of a species confers no further right on that animal, and its rights not to be harmed must be weighed equitably with the rights of any others who have this right. If, in a prevention situation, we had to choose between saving the last two members of an endangered species or saving

another individual who belonged to a species that was plentiful but whose death would be a greater prima facie harm to that individual than the harm that death would be to the two, then the rights view requires that we save that individual (Regan 1983, p. 359).

Callicott (1989) argued that Regan had not considered that the vast majority of endangered species were in fact plants and insects and neither group could claim 'subjects-of-a-life' status according to Regan's criteria. Callicott suggested that if one had to choose between protecting the last two individuals of an endangered plant species from grazing by a starving rabbit (a plentiful species), then Regan would argue that the rights of the rabbit (a mammal) must override the absence of rights of the endangered plants.

Such a moral viewpoint advocating rights only for mammals is not a workable ethic for use in modern biology and has largely been set aside in contemporary debate.

ETHICS: ROOM FOR EMOTION?

Empathy

So why can philosophers not agree? Are all animals worthy of moral consideration? What about just sentient ones? But then where does sentience begin? How are we supposed to form a belief if the professionals cannot?

In an important contribution to ethical debate, Lori Gruen (1991) hinted that the apparent lack of agreement among philosophers perhaps was based on their use of reason *in the absence of emotion*. Gruen proposed that although any argument based solely on emotion was not able to be defended morally, it was also plausible that any ethical stance based exclusively on reason may be equally invalid. John Fisher (1987), too, has advocated that difficulties in arriving at agreement on the moral status of animals may have been exacerbated by not considering the concept of sympathy. He argued simply that any being worthy of sympathy must also be worthy of moral consideration:

> One of the most important reasons why sympathy is of interest to moral theory lies in the way that it determines the range of application of our moral intuitions. Our sympathetic response to animals makes

them a part of our moral community; that is, our moral concerns and our ideas of right and wrong action extend to animals as well as to fellow humans (Fisher 1987, p. 199).

This is especially relevant for animal researchers. If we agree that scientists, as moral stewards (see below), have obligations to their experimental subjects, but that no-one is absolutely sure where such responsibilities begin and end, how may we define appropriate behaviour or proper human conduct? In short, what must we do to derive an ethic of animal experimentation? Feeling sympathy with (or, perhaps, empathy for) the subjects of our research is a concern born of emotionality, *but* scientific objectivity demands a rigorous *rational* approach to experimentation. This must create a tension between one's personal beliefs and one's professional behaviour. Might not such a tension be seen as beneficial when viewed within the framework of a universal ethic which has room for both rationality and emotionality? Such a framework is found in Albert Schweitzer's ethic of *der Ehrfurcht vor dem Leben*, or *reverence for life*.

Reverence for life

Albert Schweitzer (1875–1965), Nobel Peace Laureate, medical practitioner, doctor of philosophy and theology, was committed to developing a universal ethic which could incorporate emotionality, but which would be based on logic. Instead, in a flash of insight, he realised that the opposite would be the case: an ethic which advocated goodness towards all life, not just to humanity, would be derived not from rational thought, but from emotion:

> Certain truths originate in feeling, others in the mind. Those truths that we derive from our emotions are of a moral kind – compassion, kindness, forgiveness. Reason, on the other hand, teaches us the truths that come from reflection...The problem presented itself to me in these terms: must we really be condemned to live in this dualism of emotional and rational truths?...does the mind, in its striving for a morality that can guide us in life, lag so far behind the morality that emotion reveals because it is not sufficiently profound to be able to conceive what the great teachers, in obedience to feeling, have made known to us?

This led me to devote myself entirely to the search for a fundamental principle of morality... I had to consider the question of what the fundamental idea of existence is. What is the mind's point of departure when it sets itself to the task of reflecting on humanity and on the world in which we live? This point of departure, I said to myself, is not any knowledge of the world that we have acquired. We do not have – and we will never have – true knowledge of the world; such knowledge will always remain a mystery to us.

The point of departure naturally offered for meditation between ourselves and the world is the simple evidence that *we are life that wishes to live and are animated by a will in the midst of other lives animated by the same will.* Simply by considering the act of thinking, our consciousness tells us this. True knowledge of the world consists in our being penetrated by a sense of the mystery of existence and of life.

If we proceed on the basis of this knowledge, it is no longer isolated reason that devotes itself to thought, but our whole being, that *unity of emotion and reflection that constitutes the individual* (excerpt from radio interview, Radio Brazzaville (1955), cited in Brabazon 1976, pp. 245–6: my italics).

Schweitzer's 'revelation' led to his writing of *Civilization and Ethics* (1955). It contained the fundamental principle which was, henceforth, to govern all of his actions - reverence for life. This was an ethic which affirmed for him the position of the human species in the universe. This is further emphasised in *My Life and Thought*:

The most immediate fact of man's consciousness is the assertion: I am life which wills to live in the midst of life which wills to live... If man affirms his will-to-live, he acts naturally and honestly ... [he] feels a compulsion to give to every will-to-live the same reverence for life that he gives to his own ... He accepts as being good: to preserve life, to promote life, to raise to its highest value life which is capable of development (Schweitzer 1966, pp. 130–1).

Reverence for life is a creed which makes no distinction between 'higher' and 'lower' life forms; no distinction between plants and animals; no distinction between human beings and non-human beings. An acceptance of such an ethic does not mean that causing the death of another creature is wrong, it is the causing of pain or death *when it can be avoided* that is wrong. Anyone guided by 'reverence for life' will only cause the death or suffering of any animal in cases of *inescapable necessity*, never from thoughtlessness. For Schweitzer, this had particular relevance for the animal researcher:

> Those who experiment with operations or the use of drugs upon animals, or inoculate them with diseases, so as to be able to bring help to mankind with the results gained, must never quiet misgivings they feel with the general reflection that their cruel proceedings aim at a valuable result. They must first have considered in each individual case whether there is a real necessity to force upon any animal this sacrifice for the sake of mankind. And they must take the most anxious care to mitigate as much as possible the pain inflicted (Schweitzer 1936, p. 252).

It is worth noting here that the use of the English word 'reverence' does not necessarily carry the full meaning of the German noun *Ehrfurcht*. James Brabazon (1976) doubted that 'reverence' instilled a full sense of mystical awe. He suggested that *Ehrfurcht* was ultimate respect, and should instil in us the sorts of feelings that we experience, for example, on top of mountains or in storms at sea. Put simply, a sense of the numinous.

Schweitzer's ethic is essentially theological, and has been criticised as being too simplistic for a world view, and impractical in any reasoned discussion of animal experimentation (Flemming 1984; Anon. 1992). Peter Singer (1979) has pointed out that Schweitzer, as a physician, would have had little compunction in killing lower life forms, such as bacteria and parasites, in his treatment of patients. However, I would argue that Singer's criticism does not apply in any practical sense in the discussion of animal experimentation. Debate (and the focus of this book) is concentrated essentially on the welfare of those animals which are generally accepted as sentient beings (i.e. the animals with which we most empathise). This is reflected in the laws which govern experiments in western countries (see Chapter 5): they only apply to such clearly sentient animals. Researchers who experiment on creatures not considered sentient (i.e. all invertebrates except certain cephalopods) are not answerable to animal experimentation ethics committees or government inspectors. These laws mirror the fact that, for most people, concern for the welfare of animals in experiments is hierarchical. Moral indignation and public outcry are invariably heightened when debate turns from, say, a discussion of the welfare of gut fauna or insects to one of cats, dogs or primates.

This is not to say that researchers using invertebrates need not necessarily operate under the same ethic. Anyone who has observed the behaviour of an octopus will understand that it is not only vertebrates that are sentient:

> ...the octopus, a mollusc, is much closer genetically to a snail than a mouse is to me [but] appears to have a lot to communicate. If I approach an octopus, it looks at me, dilates its pupils, raises goose bumps on its skin, blushes and goes white and, if I persist, squirts ink at me... (Wall 1992, p. 1).

Recent concern for the welfare of the octopuses in scientific research has resulted in an amendment to the UK *Animals (Scientific Procedures) Act*, 1986 to include legal protection for *Octopus vulgaris* (Australian and New Zealand Council for the Care of Animals in Research and Teaching 1993b). Similar protection is offered in Canada to octopuses and squid (Wong 1995).

It is also interesting to note that in 1881 Charles Darwin ([1881] 1985) wrote an entire book on intelligence in earthworms, believing them to be able to make decisions in mazes. Did Darwin, perhaps, recognise that the demarcation between intelligent and non-intelligent animals may have less to do with the presence of a backbone than is generally believed? Our demarcation between vertebrates and invertebrates is a relatively recent taxonomic division. Intelligence was never a consideration when this division was made.

Eisemann *et al.* (1984, p. 167) discussed whether insects were capable of experiencing pain and concluded that entomologists ought to inactivate insect nervous systems prior to trauma. In so doing, their subjects are not only easier to handle, but it instils in the researcher:

> ...an appropriately respectful attitude towards living organisms whose physiology, though different, and perhaps simpler than our own, is as yet far from completely understood.

Singer (1993) argued that only *sentient* animals must be given an equality of consideration – a rational argument. Schweitzer urged that *all* life must be afforded the same respect: the need for every experiment must be carefully reasoned based on the ideal of reverence for life, not sentience – an argument that gives a place to emotion. Both points of view are entirely valid in the choosing of an ethic to govern animal experimentation. The Schweitzerian ideal, perhaps, has the potential to include the animals which are excluded by Singer's sentience cut-off in the event that public pressure was to increase for the inclusion of more invertebrates to be covered by the legislative umbrella governing animal experiments.

David Porter (1992, p. 101) courageously suggested all scientists adopting the 'Schweitzerian' model may become '... anti-vivisectionists at heart'. The adoption of such an ethical stance would lead to the deliberate creation of tension between one's work and one's values. Porter (1992, p. 101) admitted that many researchers would find this an outrageous scenario, but emphasised that the '... onus is on them to explain why [scientists] would not want to share an ideal that seeks always to minimise or avoid the harm we inflict on sentient animals'.

MORAL STEWARDSHIP

The four moral arguments described above, though helpful in the formation of an acceptable ethic of animal experimentation, tend to drift further and further away from the day-to-day reality of modern experimental procedures. Philosophers urge that the ability to make moral decisions ought to be an essential criterion in today's scientist. Few would disagree, and yet one is left with the notion that, in the absence of an all-encompassing ethic of animal experimentation, there is little that is clear-cut and much that is various shades of grey. Another solution? Margaret Stone (1989, pp. 30–1), an academic lawyer who gave evidence before the Australian Government's Senate Select Committee on Animal Welfare (1989), was critical of the ability of any general moral principle to answer specific questions about what to do in individual cases of animal experimentation. For her, pragmatism was of far greater importance than finding a universally applicable ethic for use when considering research animals:

> ... there are no simple answers to be found and there is no single guiding principle that will answer the questions that are raised about the

problems of animal welfare and the use of animals in our society. There have been...laudable attempts, which have had very many beneficial results, to provide such a principle but they have all failed. One reason why they have failed...is that where ethical principles are concerned, there is no possibility of proving the validity of an ethical principle and that a single principle does not take account of what I would see as the competing interests of humans and animals...So it seems to me that we have to move on very quickly from that ill-fated search to find a single principle and get down to the nitty-gritty of trying to resolve problems that arise in particular instances. (Stone, cited in Australian Government Senate Select Committee on Animal Welfare 1989, pp. 30–1).

A multidisciplinary working party convened by the British Institute of Medical Ethics (Smith and Boyd 1991) reviewed contemporary philosophical and moral debate about animal experimentation and arrived at the same conclusion. This committee consisted of veterinarians, scientists, moral philosophers and animal-welfare group representatives. They agreed that if the current discrimination between humans and other animals as research subjects was justifiable, then a *relevant* difference between the moral status of humans and non-humans must be (a) alleged and (b) morally supported. Despite extensive and rigorous philosophical debate, they were unable to find agreement among philosophers on whether any difference between humans and non-humans *could* be supported morally:

> In the light of these conclusions, it is not surprising that the multidisciplinary Working Party responsible for this study is unable to offer arguments for or against the use of animals in biomedical research to which philosophers will not take exception (Smith and Boyd 1991, p. 306).

In the absence of a keenly sought universal ethic of animal experimentation, sensible animal welfarists, both within science and without, have plotted a different course: many now recognise that animal researchers have a role as *moral stewards*. They do not object to animal experiments in situations where the research subjects are treated humanely and the experiments are justifiable because they contribute to the preservation or enhancement of human or non-human life. In this context, animal experimentation is viewed as a 'necessary evil' (Smith and Boyd 1991, p. 345), which is justifiable as long as those who conduct the experiments are in tune with their moral obligations – to society *and* to the animals in their care.

For supporters of moral stewardship, what has been established beyond doubt is that:

> ... human beings bear the burden of ... respecting and protecting the interests and welfare of those creatures which are alive and do have minimal levels of sentience ... Both the capacity for a full mental life and the ability to suffer place demands on the responsible moral [steward] that are sufficient in themselves to demand compliance and discharge. Animals deserve no less respect than that which we accord the most helpless and vulnerable members of our own species (Caplan, cited in Australian Government Senate Select Committee on Animal Welfare 1989, p. 41).

SUMMARY

We have examined several moral standpoints which involve our treatment of non-human beings in general, and research animals in particular. The first, essentially Kantian, ethic justifies our current use of non-human animals based on a human uniqueness; the second, third and fourth points of view of Singer, Regan and Schweitzer, respectively, argue strongly for an expansion of our moral circle, but for different reasons. Many variations on this theme have been put forward in the past 25 years. Most of these ideas have merit of some kind, but none of them is sufficiently all-encompassing to make a decision about the moral value of all animals a simple one.

Irrespective of whether their particular moral stance holds in every case, it would be unfair to discount the contributions made by Peter Singer and others in elevating debate and drawing public attention to the conditions under which research involving animals was conducted. Most researchers using animals now recognise that they have to work within a moral framework determined by society as a whole, not exclusively by scientists.

The issues involved in the determination of the moral status of non-human animals are complex – yet they are at the heart of the animal experimentation debate. Each reader must attempt to form an opinion of his or her own about the extent to which we use research animals. To do so is not a simple task – it will involve rational discussion and personal feelings. Many of you would have serious misgivings if asked to dissect a cat or a dog in a practical class. Fewer have the same misgivings when dealing with other animals, say, rats and mice. Yet, are not the rodents worthy of the same consideration?

Animal experimentation has been termed 'a necessary evil' (Smith and Boyd 1991, p. 345); an 'inescapable necessity' is, perhaps, less judgemental. It has numerous benefits for human and non-human health; it assists in the accumulation of information necessary for species conservation in a world of dwindling natural habitat; and it provides western society with an array of commercial products, such as shampoos and cosmetics, that consumers demand are safe for human use. At the same time, it causes pain and stress for millions of non-human animals, whether purpose-bred, captured from the wild, or collected as unwanted pets.

If viewed as an 'inescapable necessity', questions can be asked immediately about how we can reduce the level of suffering inherent in some experiments. Are there alternatives to some procedures? Can we reduce the number of experiments of dubious value? Such questions are addressed in Chapters 5 and 6.

5   Animal use and the regulation of experiments

> Where there is no scientifically and morally acceptable alternative, some use of animals in biomedical research can be justified (albeit by different moral reasons for different people) as necessary to safeguard and improve the health, and to alleviate the suffering, of human beings and [other] animals; as well as to advance fundamental scientific knowledge, upon which such therapeutic and practical benefits might depend. Such a justification, however, should be considered very carefully indeed.
>
> *Smith and Boyd (1991, p. 329)*

HOW ARE ANIMALS USED?

At the end of Chapter 2, a list is given of some of the numerous medical advances that had been made through research involving animals. It is not just the field of medicine in which such strides have been made and it is worthwhile to consider more fully the extent to which animals are used.

Fundamental and applied biological research

Fundamental, or pure, research aims to advance knowledge without having specific aims, such as an improvement in human and non-human health, in mind. Francis Bacon (1561–1626) eloquently described such research as *experimenta lucifera*, or 'experiments which shed light'. In contrast, *experimenta fructifera* described 'experiments which yield fruit' (Paton 1993). Today's term for goal-directed experimentation is 'applied research'. In practice, pure and applied research are often inextricably linked. Fundamental investigations often result in practical applications, while applied efforts often lead into new areas of fundamental research.

In biomedicine, 'illuminating' practices include experiments designed to clarify physiological systems at the molecular and cellular levels as well as at the level of organs or whole animals. Beyond biomedicine, in zoological studies for example, fundamental research may include field-

based studies of wild animal behaviour with a view to a greater understanding of biological processes or ecological interactions. Basic information of this kind may then be applied to determine an effective and
humane way of controlling particular wildlife species which may have
become pests, or to conserve threatened species.

In applied biomedical research, animals are used in many ways.
Sometimes, a particular non-human species may be found which can act
as an accurate model of a human disease. Research efforts then may be
expanded to include experimentation with this species to complement
on-going research involving humans. One such example is Pompe's disease (generalised glycogenosis, type II), an inherited, lethal, lysosomal
storage disease afflicting some human infants in their first year of life. In
Western Australia, a herd of Shorthorn cattle was found to produce
calves with generalised glycogenosis, type II. Affected calves showed
syndromes similar to those observed in clinically ill human sufferers (Di
Marco, Howell and Dorling 1984). These animals provided an opportunity to determine ante-natal and post-natal changes associated with the
disease in humans and were used to develop enzyme replacement techniques to assist in therapy and prevention (Howell, Dorling and Cook
1983).

In other applied studies, organs may be required from experimental
animals, or animals might be needed to test the efficiency and safety of
vaccines. For example, in the first half of the twentieth century, monkeys
were integral to the research which resulted in the development of a vaccine against poliomyelitis. Polio is an infectious viral disease which
causes paralysis and muscle wastage in children. In 1909, scientists had
discovered that the polio virus was transferable to some species of monkeys (Flexner and Lewis 1909). This meant that many investigations
which, for contemporary ethical reasons, could not be conducted using
human subjects could now proceed with monkeys. Forty years later,
research had advanced to the stage where researchers successfully cultured the virus on human tissue (Enders, Weller and Robbins 1949).
This led to a vaccine being released in 1955. Its effect in reducing the
number of polio cases has been spectacular. During a polio epidemic in
1952, 58 000 cases were reported in the USA. In 1984, only four cases
were recorded throughout the USA (US Congress, Office of Technology

Assessment 1986). In order to mass produce the vaccine, monkey kidney tissue was needed to produce large quantities of the virus. This meant that many monkeys were sacrificed for their kidneys. Other live monkeys were necessary to test the safety of the vaccine. Today, monkeys are no longer used in the propagation of viruses for vaccine production, although they are still used in safety testing (US Congress, Office of Technology Assessment 1986).

Behavioural research

Behavioural researchers may use animals in order to understand more completely human psychological phenomena. Animals have been used in diverse research areas including depression, drug addiction, aggressive behaviour, communication, learning and problem solving, normal and abnormal social behaviour, reproduction and parental care. Such research varies widely in its effects on the animals themselves. Experiments may be as innocuous as the non-intrusive study of behaviour in wild animals or, for instance, observing the responses of free-living vervet monkeys to the playback of taped intraspecific alarm calls (Seyfarth, Cheney and Marler 1980). Conversely, some animals have been subjected to repeated exposure to painful stimuli, such as inescapable electric shock, or have been harmed psychologically in experiments examining the effects of maternal deprivation (Rowan 1984; Stephens 1986).

Animal use in education and training

The majority of students are exposed to animals and animal dissection at some stage during their schooling. Primary education may offer opportunities for children to interact with small animals (usually mammals and birds) and so develop a positive attitude towards them. Students are encouraged to care for classroom pets and to observe general behaviour patterns. During secondary schooling, students may be exposed to animal dissection using amphibians or rodents. Senior high-school students may even conduct non-invasive behavioural experiments of their own using, for example, finches or white mice. An education which includes exposure to the humane care of animals may have positive effects later, when most university life science students are exposed to animal experimentation. As undergraduates, they may find themselves actively experimenting with animals of varying sentience, to gain knowledge and to acquire specialised skills. Involvement in experimentation will vary depending on the course in which a student is enrolled. Students of the medical and allied health professions (e.g. physiotherapy, dentistry) as well as veterinary and agricultural science students usually receive a 'vocational' training. As such, experiments using animals will be restricted to those which illustrate a particular concept or identify a particular physiological system. Students of more 'research-orientated' professions (e.g. physiology, zoology, pharmacology, biochemistry and psychology) use animals as 'tools' in solving research problems or answering questions about the natural world. The particular use of animals will vary from course to course depending on which research principle or biological concept is being taught.

Production of useful biological and therapeutic materials

Animals are also used in the evaluation of drugs intended for medical or veterinary use, and for the production of useful biological substances. For example, monoclonal antibodies are raised in a variety of animals for use in diagnostic immunological procedures. Similarly, some animals, often horses, are used in the production of anti-venenes used to treat snake bite victims (human and non-human).

Animal use in product testing

Beyond scientific inquiry and education, laboratory animals are used to test consumables in the interests of user safety. Government regulatory agencies often require that such products (chemicals, pharmaceuticals and cosmetics, mainly) be tested before they are released for general use. Animals are used in testing. The US Congress, Office of Technology Assessment (1986) listed among such tests, the following:

- *Acute toxicity tests* consisting of the administration of a single dose of a chemical at a concentration great enough to produce toxic effects and death. An example of such a test is the Lethal Dose 50 (LD50) test in which 50 per cent of the subjects in an experimental sample are expected to die.

- *Biological screening tests* designed to determine the biological activity of organic compounds in experimental animals.
- *Carcinogenicity tests* where animals, usually rodents, are exposed repeatedly during their life to potential carcinogens (cancer-causing agents).
- *Developmental and reproductive toxicity tests* consisting of several procedures designed to assess the potential of chemicals to induce miscarriages or to cause infertility or birth defects, usually in rodents and rabbits.
- *Eye and skin irritation tests* designed to determine whether a particular chemical or product will cause irritation on handling or exposure. The notorious Draize Test (Draize, Woodward and Calvery 1944), in which rabbits have test substances dripped into one eye (the other acts as a control), is an example.
- *Mutagenicity tests* designed to assess whether certain products are capable of causing genetic mutations.
- *Neurotoxicity tests* to determine the extent of toxic effects on vertebrate nervous systems. Animal behaviour is observed to detect any lack of co-ordination, motor disorders, altered learning abilities or gross behavioural changes.
- *Repeated-dose chronic toxicity tests* commonly use rodents to test the effects of repeated exposure (2 weeks to 12 months) to particular chemicals.

THE REGULATION OF EXPERIMENTS

As already noted, animals are integral to many areas of modern science, education and product testing. Western societies insist on the thorough regulation of all such uses and this has been done, albeit in different ways in different countries, with considerable success. That does not mean, of course, that there is not room for improvement. Some countries lag behind other nations that have more progressive legislation that accords protection to a wider range of species (e.g. Australia, Britain, Canada and the USA).

While it is beyond the scope of this book to review all statutes in all nations that have laboratory animal welfare legislation, it is worthwhile to contrast three regulatory approaches: the British centralised government inspectorate system, the US self-regulation system, and the enforced self-regulation system of Australia and New Zealand that establishes Animal Experimentation Ethics Committees (AEECs). By examining each system, the extent of legal cover can be explored and the opportunity for further protection canvassed. Readers interested in a more thorough review of all western regulations are referred to comprehensive discussions elsewhere (Hampson 1989; Orlans 1993; Hamm, Dell and Van Sluyters 1995; Institute of Laboratory Animal Resources 1995; Rollin 1995; Wilkins 1997; Hart 1998; Paver 1998; Straughan and Balls 1998).

United Kingdom

The UK *Animals (Scientific Procedures) Act* (1986) is administered through the British Home Office, which produces publicly available annual reports that detail aspects of experimentation conducted under the Act (UK Home Office 1999). The UK Act offers strict protection for all living vertebrates as well as for the common octopus, *Octopus vulgaris*. It controls animal research in the following ways:

1. certification and licensing of researchers and their projects
2. institutional certification
3. enforcement through the Home Office inspectorate
4. the establishment of an Animal Procedures Committee.

In so doing, it offers laboratory animals four tiers of protection. Researchers and other responsible individuals who breach the UK Act are guilty of criminal offences.

Certification and licensing

Personal and project licences are given to researchers by the British Home Secretary provided they work within an institution that has a Certificate of Designation. This certificate is given to universities or other research establishments once it has been demonstrated that the institution is a suitable place in which research can be conducted and that the welfare of animals is of concern before, during and after an experiment. Personal licences are given to researchers that can demonstrate, following a period of supervision, an appropriate level of aptitude in specified techniques using designated species. The project licence sets out specifically what can be done as part of any experimental procedure(s), for example collecting blood or drug administration. It limits the severity of experimental endpoints (mild, moderate, substantial) based on perceived benefits. An experiment with minor costs to an animal in terms of suffering but with substantial potential benefits is more likely to be licensed than a procedure where the opposite is the case.

Institutional certification

An institutional Certificate of Designation is held by a senior individual (e.g. a university vice-chancellor) who is responsible for ensuring that all experimentation falls within the purview of the UK Act. This individual is responsible for appointing named veterinarians and named day-to-day care personnel for projects conducted within the institution. It is his or her responsibility to ensure the welfare of animals held within the institution.

The Home Office inspectorate

The Home Secretary appoints Home Office inspectors who have three principal duties. First, to consider in detail all licence applications and to advise the Home Secretary how to ensure that only properly justified research is conducted. Second, to carry out episodic visits to institutions holding Certificates of Designation each year to ensure that licence terms and conditions are being met. Finally, as trained medical or veterinary personnel with knowledge of the administration of the UK Act, inspectors are able to give expert advice and assistance to licensees and other personnel.

The Animal Procedures Committee

This committee consists of practising scientists, lay and welfare representatives as well as at least one person trained in law. It has the power to make broad judgements and recommendations to the Home Office about issues in animal experimentation and to advise the government about matters concerning the UK Act. The committee reviews all project licences in some categories (e.g. tobacco research, cosmetic testing) and has the power to review any other project licence. At least two-thirds of the committee must be scientists, physicians or veterinarians, and at least half of the committee must consist of non-practising experimenters. The proportion of animal welfare representatives on the committee is unstated under the UK Act other than that they be 'adequately represented'.

These four tiers of control emphasise personal responsibility for laboratory animals and the procedures in which they are used, and are generally accepted by those who work within the UK Act as fair and sensible. However, as this book goes to print, there is no reference to AEECs within the UK Act, and final decisions about what is and is not appropriate conduct within a research institution are taken by the Home Office inspectors (approximately 25 individuals throughout Britain). This has been criticised because, although they have scientific training, inspectors have been given no formal instruction in ethics. This may lead to them having a biased view in favour of experimentation (Townsend and Morton 1995). It is also unlikely that 25 or so inspectors adequately represent or reflect an evolving public attitude to experimentation. Recognition of this has resulted in the UK government introducing a requirement for all establishments conducting research involving live animals to institute an ethical review process. It is highly likely that this process will involve the enabling of AEECs with a similar role to such committees in Australia, the USA and elsewhere.

United States of America

The US model differs from the British and Australasian systems in that certain vertebrates are currently excluded from protection under government legislation (the Federal *Animal Welfare Act*). This exclusion has led to a number of organisations, both government and non-government, having responsibility for affording protection to all vertebrates used in experiments. Under the *Animal Welfare Act*, animals are defined as:

> ... any live or dead dog, cat, nonhuman primate, guinea pig, hamster, rabbit, or any other warm-blooded animal, which is being used, or is intended for use in research, teaching, testing, experimentation, or exhibition purposes, or as a pet (cited in Hamm *et al.* 1995).

Following amendment in 1971, the Act now specifically excludes:

...birds, rats of the genus *Rattus* and mice of the genus *Mus* bred for use in research, and horses not used for research purposes and other farm animals...used or intended for use as food or fiber or...for improving animal nutrition, breeding, management, or production efficiency, or for improving the quality of food or fiber (cited in Hamm *et al.* 1995).

This could be argued as a weakness of the US system, since the majority of US experiments involve purpose-bred rodents (up to 17 million per year: Mukerjee 1997) that have no legislative protection. Also excluded by definition are all birds and cold-blooded animals (frogs, toads, salamanders and reptiles) used in research. Attempts to have all vertebrates included under the *Animal Welfare Act* have failed, although the US Department of Agriculture (the USDA, which administers the Act) is due to review the Act again early in the twenty-first century (Mukerjee 1997).

In the absence of all-encompassing legislative protection, the US system involves a system of government and non-government organisations all aiming to ensure that the welfare of experimental animals is uppermost. In separate circumstances, each organisation has strong powers to suspend funding, shut down laboratories or withdraw accreditation from research facilities that do not comply with welfare regulations. It is worthwhile to examine the roles of three major institutions better to understand how the US system protects its research animals from abuse. These are Institutional Animal Care and Use Committees (IACUCs) established by the *Animal Welfare Act*, the National Institute of Health (NIH) Office of Protection from Research Risks that oversees all NIH-funded research, and the Association for Assessment and Accreditation of Laboratory Animal Care International (AAALAC International), a private organisation that accredits only research laboratories that pursue the highest standards of laboratory animal care.

Institutional Animal Care and Use Committees

Two broadly complementary federal laws, the *Animal Welfare Act* and the *Health Research Extension Act*, are implemented by regulations stated in the Code of Federal regulations and the Public Health Service (PHS) Policy on Humane Care and Use of Laboratory Animals, respectively. It is the PHS policy, together with the *Animal Welfare Act*, that establishes IACUCs. Each research facility, whether public or private, has its own committee, and the PHS policy requires each establishment to adhere to the *Guide for the Care and Use of Laboratory Animals* (National Research Council 1996). IACUCs must have a minimum of five members to comply with PHS policy, of which at least one member must not be affiliated with the institution and should reflect general community views (Hamm *et al.* 1995). In reality, many research facilities have ten or more members on their committee. Each IACUC performs a six-monthly review of the animal care and use programme and animal-house facilities, using the NRC guide (1996) as an evaluation base using USDA inspectors. IACUC members are also responsible for reviewing all research protocols prior to their commencement and for reviewing any concerns that may arise during the conduct of research. IACUCs have significant stated responsibilities that require research facilities to provide appropriate veterinary care and preoperative and postoperative attention (including the appropriate use of analgesics). An IACUC is authorised to suspend any research that is being conducted outside of the approved protocol.

The National Institute of Health

The NIH funds a significant proportion of animal-based research in the USA. It regulates animal experimentation in both the private and public sectors (e.g. universities) through its Office for Protection from Research Risks. The NIH regulations cover all vertebrates including rodents, reptiles and birds. This means that if research is conducted in a university laboratory (or a private laboratory receiving NIH funding), then researchers or laboratories must comply with NIH regulations as well as with those established by the *Animal Welfare Act* and administered by IACUCs. Failure to meet strict NIH criteria may result in the suspension of all funding and laboratories being closed down. In many respects, the NIH regulations are stronger than those established by the *Animal Welfare Act*.

Association for Assessment and Accreditation of Laboratory Animal Care International

AAALAC International is a private organisation that has conducted a voluntary accreditation programme for laboratories using animals since its inception[1] in 1965. AAALAC International uses performance standards to evaluate and accredit research facilities and institutions (Bayne and Martin 1998). It's regulations are more strict than NIH and USDA regulations, meaning that research organisations with an AAALAC International 'seal of approval' are of the highest standard when it comes to laboratory animal welfare. The NIH and the National Science Foundation both view AAALAC International accreditation as evidence of exemplary standards of laboratory animal care. Increasingly, this means that for a research establishment to gain funding for experimentation in a competitive environment, it must seek and maintain AAALAC International accreditation.

Australia and New Zealand

The regulation of animal experimentation in Australia and New Zealand also differs considerably from the UK model. Rather than centralised government administration on a day-to-day basis, these nations operate a form of enforced self-regulation using institutional AEECs. Indeed, Australia has no federal legislation which oversees animal experimentation at all. Responsibility for the proper conduct of animal researchers in universities, hospitals, industry and agriculture lies with each state or territory. All states and territories have some form of prevention of cruelty to animals legislation (e.g. the Victorian *Prevention of Cruelty to Animals Act,* 1986). These laws were enacted at various times during the twentieth century and are updated periodically to reflect changes in community concerns. The most recent updates have taken into consideration animals used in experiments and have incorporated adherence to a national code of practice, *The Australian Code of Practice for the Care and Use of Animals for Scientific Purposes.* This is an evolving code that was first produced by the Australian National Health and Medical Research Council (NHMRC) in 1969. *The Australian Code of Practice* is currently in its sixth edition (National Health and Medical Research Council 1997). It aims to ensure the humane care of non-human vertebrates used for scientific, educational and testing purposes. It does this by:

[1]Prior to 1996, AAALAC International was known as the American Association for Accreditation of Laboratory Animal Care

- emphasising the responsibilities of both the scientists and/or educators using animals and the institutions in which the work is conducted;
- ensuring that the welfare of animals is treated as a priority;
- ensuring that all experimental, testing and teaching procedures are justified within the 'three Rs' principles of Russell and Burch (1959);
- minimising the numbers of animals used, and limiting or avoiding pain or distress;
- actively promoting the use of techniques which replace animal experiments.

The Australian Code of Practice establishes, and acts as a practical guide for, institutional AEECs. Committees consist of at least four people with expertise in separate areas: first, a qualified veterinarian; second, a person with recent experience in animal experimentation; third, a person committed to advancing the welfare of animals (and who is not employed by the institution); fourth, a person independent of the institution who has never had anything to do with animal experimentation.

The regulation of experiments in New Zealand works in a similar way. The New Zealand *Animals Protection (Codes of Ethical Conduct) Regulations* (1987) govern what researchers can, and cannot, do using animals in their care. The New Zealand model differs slightly from its Australian counterpart in that each research institution derives its own code of ethical conduct and approval is then sought for each institutional code from the New Zealand National Animal Ethics Advisory Committee. No experiments are permitted to proceed prior to approval being gained. At least six people sit on each institutional AEEC: three from within the institution and three independent members. One independent member is a veterinarian nominated by the NZ Veterinary Association, one represents a recognised animal welfare group (usually the RNZSPCA) and one is a lay person with no scientific affiliations.

The New Zealand equivalent of the *Australian Code of Practice* is the *Code of Recommendations and Minimum Standards for the Care and Use of Animals for Scientific Purposes*, developed by the NZ Animal Welfare Advisory Committee.

There are presently over 200 AEECs in Australia and New Zealand.

People who wish to conduct research using animals, whether it be an undergraduate rat or toad dissection or complex surgery involving kangaroos or primates, must first seek the approval of their AEEC. To do this, they must submit a written proposal which includes:

- explicit and achievable aims;
- details of expected benefits flowing from their work;
- details of the vertebrate species to be used;
- consideration of the expected impact on the experimental subjects, and evidence that a cost–benefit analysis, with said impact in mind, has been done;
- evidence that the experimental design is adequate to demonstrate the stated aims;
- details of the ways in which pain and suffering will be alleviated or eliminated before, during and after the planned procedure.

In addition, there is a growing trend for scientists to indicate what alternatives to the use of live animals have been considered during the preparation of AEEC applications.

The AEEC then considers, and approves, modifies or rejects the proposal. Long-term research is reviewed annually. With this structure in place, it should not be possible for a poorly thought out or non-achievable experiment to be conducted. Scientists know that their work will not be permitted to proceed unless they have given thorough consideration to the welfare of animals in their care.

Summary

The British and Australasian systems represent opposite ends of a regulation spectrum. In the first case, research animals are given a high level of protection based on personal responsibility and criminal sanctions overseen by government representatives. In the latter case, research animals are provided with similar levels of protection through institutional AEECs and enforced self-regulation. Each committee has lay and welfare representatives who are in the best position to assert contemporary public opinion about issues in animal experimentation. This means that an experiment with ethical costs approved today may not necessarily be approved tomorrow if popular consensus (reflected on the committee) shifts. In the UK system prior to 1999, the Home Office inspectors acted as 'one-person AEECs' (Townsend and Morton 1995) and it is difficult to see how this system could adequately reflect evolving public attitudes towards animal experimentation in the same way as with Australian and New Zealand AEECs. In recognition of this, the Home Secretary now requires each research facility to initiate an ethical review process.

The US model is more closely aligned to the Australasian system than it is to the UK model. Through IACUCs, an acceptable standard of housing and husbandry is enforced, although the *Animal Welfare Act* does not accord legislative protection to all vertebrates. Failure to offer legislative protection to birds, amphibians, reptiles, purpose-bred rodents and livestock used in research has resulted in a complex arrangement whereby government agencies such as the NIH, the PHS and the USDA all have varying powers to control ethical conduct within laboratories. Overlying this system is a private regulatory authority, AAALAC International, that offers accreditation only to facilities where laboratory animal care is of the highest standard.

This mix of public and private regulation may be viewed as a result of the *Animal Welfare Act*'s failure to give legislative protection to all vertebrates. As it stands, though, the complex administrative mix summarised here can be seen to work. Research in public institutions is very highly regulated by the NIH, with strict sanctions able to be enforced in cases where laboratory animal care is lax. In the private sector, marketplace competition may dictate the necessity for companies that conduct (or rely on) animal research and testing to have (or to deal with research institutions that have) AAALAC International accreditation in the first instance to attract further funding and, in the second case, to demonstrate a commitment to animal welfare to its increasingly informed and concerned customers.

6   Seeking alternatives

Perhaps one can see a future where an animal experiment imposes no more on the animal than does domestication, and yet can be seen as providing a new fulfilment for the animal world – a companionship with man in advancing knowledge and, for both, a diminishment of future suffering.

William Paton (1993, p. 230)

INTRODUCTION

Despite enormous advancements in research animal welfare, criticism of animal experimentation remains as vociferous today as it has ever been. The past 25 years have seen a revitalisation of the animal welfare movement and a consequent proliferation of literature regarding moral, ethical or regulatory aspects of animal experimentation. After Peter Singer (1975) and Tom Regan (1983) re-stimulated debate through their professional interests in the moral status of animals and ethical aspects of animal research, advocates for the humane treatment of animals, such as Richard Ryder (1975) and Bernard Rollin (1981), chronicled many examples of modern research of dubious merit and legitimately challenged the value of results obtained from certain poorly designed experiments.

During the 1970s, 1980s and 1990s in the UK and elsewhere, there were unconscionable physical attacks on scientists, their laboratories and their families by members of an extremist fringe who believed that the cause of animal welfare could be advanced more quickly by the publicity their actions generated.

How has the scientific community responded to such challenges? Some scientists have written books in defence of their disciplines, few more persuasively than William Paton (1993). Others have been active in suggesting ways of refining and reducing experimental procedures with the welfare of laboratory animals in mind. Many researchers have offered submissions to various government inquiries as legislation has been drafted to ensure the humane treatment of research animals, or have made valuable contributions to the establishment of effective Animal Experimentation Ethics Committees (AEECs).

Around the world, organisations such as ANZCCART,[1] AWIC,[2] CCAC,[3] FRAME[4] and UFAW[5] provide guidelines for the effective conduct of animal experimentation and up-to-date information on alternatives to the use of sentient animals. In Britain, UFAW and FRAME regularly inform the scientific and wider community of the availability of new alternatives to the use of animals in experiments (e.g. Universities Federation for Animal Welfare and Fund for the Replacement of Animals in Medical Experiments 1998). UFAW produces books on the practical aspects of research animal welfare (e.g. Boyle 1991; Animal Welfare Information Center and Universities Federation for Animal Welfare 1995; Ingle 1995), and was instrumental in the pioneering of the 'three Rs' (Russell and Burch 1959). FRAME's principal function is to evaluate techniques for replacing animals in experiments as they are developed and to disseminate such information as widely as possible. This is done primarily through FRAME's journal *Alternatives to Laboratory Animals*. In Australia and New Zealand, a similar role is played by ANZCCART and *ANZCCART News*. In North America, the US AWIC and the CCAC are among the principal institutions that perform similar work. This chapter examines how such alternatives are being sought, and actively adopted.

REPLACEMENT, REDUCTION AND REFINEMENT

During the 1950s, UFAW commissioned two scientists, William Russell and Rex Burch, to prepare a manuscript detailing acceptable experimental procedures involving research animals. Their publication, *The Principles of Humane Experimental Technique* (1959), emphasised the need for scientists to appraise their work based on the principle of the

[1] Australian and New Zealand Council for the Care of Animals in Research and Teaching.
[2] Animal Welfare Information Center.
[3] Canadian Council on Animal Care.
[4] Fund for the Replacement of Animals in Medical Experiments.
[5] Universities Federation for Animal Welfare.

'three Rs'. They recommended that research efforts be directed towards the ultimate replacement of sentient animals in experiments with non-sentient or non-living alternatives at every opportunity. This was recognised as the ideal towards which all researchers should strive. In the absence of complete replacement, scientists were urged to reduce the number of experiments so that only those considered essential were performed. The number of animals used in such procedures should also be reduced as far as possible, consistent with the requirements of statistical analyses. Finally, scientists were directed to refine experiments to minimise or eliminate completely any suffering involved.

These recommendations have been accepted universally as a corner-stone of modern research practices. Indeed, in some countries, the principle of the 'three Rs' is embodied in legislation. For example, the UK *Animals (Scientific Procedures) Act* (1986) is based on the government decree that:

> ...animal experiments that are unnecessary, use unnecessarily large numbers of animals, or are unnecessarily painful, are undesirable (cited in FRAME Toxicity Committee 1991, p. 119).

Similarly, the 1986 European Community Directive No. 7.2 insists that:

> ...an experiment shall not be performed if another scientifically satis-factory method of obtaining the result sought, not entailing the use of an animal, is reasonably and practicably available (cited in FRAME Toxicity Committee 1991, p. 119).

Directive No. 7.3 states:

> When an experiment has to be performed, the choice of species shall be carefully considered and, where necessary, explained to the authority. In a choice between experiments, those which use the min-imum number of animals, involve animals with the lowest degree of neurophysiological sensitivity, cause the least pain, suffering, dis-tress or lasting harm and which are most likely to provide satisfactory results shall be selected (Balls 1990, p. 227).

There is little doubt that all concerned with the welfare of animals see the notion of the 'three Rs' as worthy. Some would argue, however, that progress towards alternatives is inexorably slow and much research should be suspended until alternatives are available. Others argue that we neglect vital research while alternatives are sought. Common sense dictates that we must actively encourage the search for alternatives while maintaining essential and humanely conducted research.

ALTERNATIVES TO NON-HUMAN VERTEBRATES IN SCIENTIFIC RESEARCH

Definitions

In each of the areas of scientific research described in Chapter 5, there is wide scope for the application of alternatives encompassing the 'three Rs' of Russell and Burch (1959). The success of such an approach to the reform of modern animal experimentation is that it does not impede the fundamental aims of scientific endeavour. Rather, it presents an essentially pro-science ideal which challenges researchers to develop afford-able and ethically superior experimental methods (Rowan 1984).

For the purposes of this discussion, alternatives to animal experiments can be usefully defined as:

> ...procedures which can completely replace the need for animal experiments, reduce the number of animals required, or diminish the amount of pain or distress suffered by the animals in meeting the essential needs of [humans] and other animals.

This is a definition which has gained wide acceptance in Europe and North America (see, for example, Balls 1983, 1990; US Congress, Office of Technology Assessment 1986; Smith and Boyd 1991).

The examples used below are widely known and proven by years of successful use. They serve to illustrate the principles of the 'three Rs'. The search for alternatives is on-going and readers are referred to the NORINA[6] database (http://oslovet.veths.no/NORINA) for updated versions available on a suite of media including CD-ROM, web-based packages and videotapes, or alternatives specific to their areas of interest.

Replacement alternatives

Replacement alternatives eliminate the use of vertebrates in particular experiments. Such methods can be classified into several categories:

[6] Norwegian Reference Centre for Laboratory Animal Science and Alternatives.

1. The use of less- (or non-) sentient organisms.
2. The use of *in-vitro* techniques.
3. The use of non-biological replacement alternatives.
4. Human studies.

The use of less- (or non-) sentient organisms (invertebrates and micro-organisms)

The presence in biological systems of broadly applicable physiological and anatomical generalisations makes it possible to substitute non-sentient life forms in experiments which might otherwise involve vertebrates. This is perhaps best illustrated by the principle of 'unity in diversity' (National Research Council 1985). Despite myriad differences between animal species, unity is evident based upon common anatomical features and the general similarity of cell function and development pathways. For example, the process of early embryonic development in all vertebrates follows the same pathway. Every vertebrate, whether a fish or a human, grows from a blastula stage and follows a genetically programmed development which includes the formation of ectodermal, mesodermal and endodermal cells. Molecular biology offers further evidence of similarities between species – the genetic code applies to all micro-organisms, plants and animals (National Research Council 1988). If invertebrates, early-stage vertebrate embryos, plants, bacteria and other micro-organisms all show common cellular and biochemical traits, then all offer the opportunity for development as alternatives to using fully developed vertebrates in experimentation.

Examples

- An alternative to the use of mammals in some experiments is a simple test which uses coelenterate hydra to detect chemicals which may produce fetal abnormalities (teratogens). This procedure is based on the observation that vertebrate teratogens also impede the normal development of hydra (Stephens 1989).
- Some invertebrates offer widespread alternatives for students in primary and secondary education. Organisms such as flatworms, earthworms, some molluscs, insects and crustaceans all may be substituted for vertebrates as simple systems of sophisticated biological phenomena.

Such organisms are not necessarily the ones with which students normally show a great deal of empathy (certain mammals generally elicit stronger bonds). However, it is a relatively simple task for teachers to emphasise common links between humans and all other creatures, or to explain why a 'lower' species is being used in preference to a 'higher' one.

The use of in-vitro techniques

In-vitro (in-glass) methods afford researchers the opportunity to study many physiological systems outside the body. Currently, technology is available which permits the culturing of cells and tissues and the maintenance of organs and organ slices in nutrient media.

Examples
- Cell, tissue or organ cultures can be used to test potentially toxic chemicals in rigidly controlled trials. Cultured cells can be observed microscopically while a suspected toxin is added. Rather than administering a drug which is thought to cause heart palpitations in vertebrates to a group of white mice, researchers can simply record changes in the beating of cultured heart cells *in-vitro* in response to the drug.
- The *Limulus* amoebocyte lysate (LAL) test is used to determine whether the intravenous administration of certain fluids to humans will cause fever. Fever-producing agents (pyrogens) were once tested on rabbits, but the LAL test means that the same results can be obtained from blood products of horseshoe crabs.
- In the pharmaceutical industry, tissue culture techniques have been used to screen potential anti-viral agents. Rather than inoculate vertebrates (usually mice) with each test substance, cell and organ cultures are utilised. One company, using 16 000 mice per year to screen 1000 potential anti-viral agents in 1963, was able to screen 22 000 substances using fewer than 2000 mice in 1975 (Stephens 1989).

In-vitro techniques have other advantages over *in-vivo* methods. Cells and tissues can be studied in an isolated environment, away from the influence of integrated physiological systems. The influence of such systems may then be mimicked under controlled conditions in further experiments. Another obvious advantage is that drugs can be tested on tissue derived from humans, thereby obviating the need for extrapolation from an animal model to the human condition.

The use of non-biological replacement alternatives

Non-biological alternatives to experiments using vertebrates currently include mathematical modelling, computer simulation and the use of audiovisual techniques for education and training. Mathematical modelling is currently being used in the active designing of pharmaceuticals for specific purposes; the modelling of biochemical, toxicological and physiological processes; and the predictive modelling known as QSAR modelling. Quantitative structure–activity relationships (QSAR) are modelled to predict potential toxic activity of chemical compounds based on molecular structure. By examining the physical parameters of molecules in a certain chemical compound, QSAR modelling enables predictions to be made about the toxicity of new compounds containing similar molecules.

Mathematical models also may be generated to predict the outcome of certain research pathways. Used in this way, such models can reduce unnecessary and wasteful research, thereby saving time, money and experimental subjects.

Computer simulation offers many opportunities for reducing the numbers of procedures involving vertebrates in education and training.

Examples

- The *Rat Stack* is an excellent example of an early training program (ACCART 1988). Rather than dissecting a rat bred and purchased for undergraduate use, students can simulate the dissection in a non-intimidatory way, at their own pace. Functional anatomy is emphasised with high resolution imaging as the student removes 'layers' from the 'stack'. Advances in computer speed and technology mean that software packages such as *The Digital Frog* CD-ROM offer similar features as well as incorporating information on behaviour, life cycle and ecology.

- Sophisticated simulations such as *MacMan, MacPuf, MacPee* and *MacDope*, developed in the 1980s at MacMaster University in Hamilton, Canada, continue to offer medical and physiology students alternative methods of coming to grips with the interactive nature of brain, heart and circulatory function, fluid physiology and the effects of pharmaceuticals.

It is unlikely that such simulations will completely replace the need for actual dissection. However, today many undergraduate science students do not follow a career in medical or biochemical research, for which it is essential that students are trained with animals.

Film and videotape presentations offer students a wide range of non-experimental options in learning. Audiovisual aids may demonstrate surgical technique or teach correct procedures for handling live animals. Although they cannot offer 'hands-on' experience, some particularly sophisticated video recordings are available.

Examples
- *Biovideograph* can be connected to a videotape player and television on which students watch an experiment being performed. A chart recorder provides a hard copy of results from the experiment and students are encouraged to analyse and interpret these data as if they had performed the experiment themselves.

The extension of non-biological alternatives may see the widespread use of computer linked mannequins to provide sophisticated simulations.
- *Resusci-Dog* is a simulator developed at Cornell University, New York, for veterinary students. It is the equivalent of the human mannequins used in the training of resuscitation techniques, but is driven by microprocessors. It can simulate a femoral artery pulse and may be used for cardiac massage. It has been reported that *Resusci-Dog* has replaced as many as 100 dogs previously used by students each year at Cornell University (US Congress, Office of Technology Assessment 1986).
- Another major advance which is predicted to replace vertebrates used in the training of biomedical scientists is *virtual reality*. State-

of-the-art computer simulation offers users an opportunity to 'perform' experiments such as laparoscopies without the need for a patient. By connecting a laparoscope to a virtual reality generator, images of what a surgeon 'sees' as he or she 'enters' a body are produced. Such technology is still in its infancy, but currently holds the potential to outstrip other simulation methods in the near future.

Human studies

A final replacement alternative worthy of consideration is the use of humans rather than other vertebrates. Tissues derived from humans *post mortem* are able to be used for many purposes. Additionally, human placentae can be used, for example, as a source of cells for tissue culture, or in the training of microsurgical techniques (US Congress, Office of Technology Assessment 1986).

Research has also been conducted using human volunteers. Under the 1975 Tokyo Amendment to the 1964 Helsinki Declaration, volunteers consent to a particular experiment after being informed of specific procedures and the inherent risks. Students of medicine, physiology and psychology are often involved in non-invasive experiments where they use one another as 'guinea-pigs'. In industry, cosmetics have been tested for potential irritancy on volunteers rather than on non-humans (Smyth 1978).

The development of new pharmaceutical agents currently involves exhaustive testing using *in-vitro* techniques, non-human vertebrates and, ultimately, human testing. Could we not move simply from *in-vitro* development to testing on volunteers, eliminating the need for research animal testing? The response to such a question rests entirely on the degree of risk society as a whole is prepared to take. It is worthwhile to consider the development of one drug, thalidomide, to assist in forming an opinion.

The tragedy of thalidomide   Thalidomide caused birth defects in children in the early 1960s after it had been prescribed to women to alleviate morning sickness early in pregnancy. It was first developed in Europe as a sedative in the mid-1950s. The manufacturer described it as structurally analogous to barbiturates, although its method of action was never investigated (National Health and Medical Research Council

1990a). Following testing in rodents, the company distributed thalido-mide to doctors, claiming it to be a rapid-acting, long-lasting sedative. No teratogenicity studies were conducted. Early reports of side-effects involving the central nervous system and a general lack of tolerance to the prescribed dose rates were ignored and, in 1957, the manufacturer released the drug onto the general non-prescription market in an influenza mixture (National Health and Medical Research Council 1990a). In 1960, there was a spate of abnormal births from mothers who had taken thalidomide early in pregnancy. Children were born with diges-tive tract abnormalities and with incompletely developed or absent limbs.

Thalidomide was withdrawn from sale in October 1961. Intensive test-ing for teratogenicity using many animal species yielded markedly vari-able results. Pregnant guinea-pigs and mice which had been dosed with thalidomide did not give birth to abnormal offspring. Rats of different strains showed varying sensitivity to thalidomide. Not all strains were sensitive and those which were reabsorbed abnormal fetuses, thus mask-ing the results of experiments designed to produce malformed young. Dogs did not show gross abnormalities, although some puppies were born with necrotic tail tips and first toes. It was not until 1962 that birth defects similar to those seen in humans were found in laboratory ani-mals. Pregnant New Zealand White rabbits dosed with thalidomide gave birth to fewer young, with increased rates of stillbirth and reduction deformities. Testing using macaques, rhesus monkeys and marmosets showed birth abnormalities similar to those seen in human babies (National Health and Medical Research Council 1990a).

What we know now, but did not know then, is that the timing during preg-nancy of the administration of a drug in a teratogenicity trial is critical. Different species have different gestation lengths, and teratogenicity effects are highly dependent on the stage of pregnancy at which a drug is given.

The tragedy of thalidomide has been used to argue both for and against the use of drug testing on non-human animals. Opponents claim that the physiologies of animals used for drug testing are sufficiently dif-ferent from human physiology for such testing to be essentially useless. Proponents of drug testing using laboratory animals use the same example of thalidomide to argue that current levels of animal use should be maintained to ensure that such a tragedy can never occur again.

Reduction alternatives

There are powerful ethical reasons for reducing the numbers of vertebrates used in experiments. Morally, it is our duty to limit any distress caused to laboratory animals during confinement or experimentation. The onus is on every researcher to justify each proposed action as the *exclusive* means to his or her desired end, to use fewer sentient animals, animals of lesser sentience, and to employ less painful procedures at every opportunity.

There are several tried and tested methods for reducing numbers of research animals. These include: pooling available resources; using the appropriate statistical techniques; and not repeating experiments unnecessarily. Well-organised research establishments hold regular seminars so that scientists are constantly kept abreast of work being conducted in other departments. Regular communication between scientists provides opportunities for pooling of resources. It makes good sense for researchers to collaborate whenever possible and to arrange for the simultaneous use of animals in more than one project. For example, if an animal has been bred or purchased for the periodic collection of blood or for tissue biopsy, it can then be used prior to euthanasia for the collection of cells for culture, or its organs may be used *post mortem* in histological investigations. If a wild animal is captured for experimentation and is to be euthanased at the end of the research, the carcass ought to be given, whenever possible, to a museum so that a taxidermist can prepare it for educative purposes. Obviously, there are many instances when the sharing of laboratory animals is not feasible, but it must be part of the modern training process that researchers constantly seek novel ways to lower the number of animals used in science.

Unnecessary repetition of experiments is best avoided by adhering to long-established scientific procedures, including the thorough searching of the technical literature, peer review prior to experimentation and the *rapid* publication of results in scientific journals. By researching one's topic thoroughly, it may be found that a particular experiment has already been conducted elsewhere. Peer review will aid in minimising the number of animals used in each procedure by directing inexperienced researchers to the appropriate statistical method when designing their experiments.

Many experiments must be repeated. In some instances, earlier results need to be checked for accuracy – particularly when new models or techniques are being developed. Reproducibility is a cornerstone of the scientific method. It is being shown increasingly in some fields that small, sometimes trivial, differences in the conditions under which an experiment is conducted can produce vastly different results. For example, we now know that many physiological systems are affected markedly by photoperiod. An experiment conducted in the morning may yield completely different results from one performed in the afternoon. It is now being found that, in certain circumstances, long-regarded 'facts' are by no means universal and may hold only under specific conditions. This has important implications for animal researchers. It is critical that any variation inherent in a system be taken into consideration when designing an experiment.

Competent scientists recognise that their careers depend on their ability to attract research funds and then to use these funds efficiently in pursuit of their goals. To this end, a great deal of thought must be given to the design of any experiment. No granting body is going to be interested in awarding financial or other resources to researchers who have not given thorough consideration to their proposed research. This is especially relevant in projects where animals are to be used: the repercussions of a 'slap happy' approach to research may be far reaching.

Research scientists must formulate their grant application with *specific* aims in mind. Applicants will be given short shrift by referees acting on behalf of a funding body if little thought is evident in this facet of experimental design. Modern experimentation demands that research aims be both *achievable* and *worthwhile*. In designing any experiment which involves animals, the first question to be addressed must be: is this experiment necessary? A thorough review of the scientific literature may often reveal similar work conducted elsewhere. Such a finding may call into question the relevance of the experimental aims, in which case, a researcher must be prepared to return to the drawing board. It is no longer acceptable that scientists expend their time (and their subjects' lives) conducting ill-conceived or already completed experiments.

Having decided that a particular project has achievable aims, the next step is to justify the research in terms of perceived benefits. Deciding whether the entire exercise is worthwhile is necessarily a subjective assessment. No one can be completely sure of the outcomes of an experiment until it has been performed. Consequently, several factors must be taken into account when assessing an experiment's relative merits.

Smith and Boyd (1991) have proposed criteria by which a project's aims ought to be judged. First, an experiment will be deemed worthwhile if it has *potential* economic, educational, scientific and/or social value. Second, one must assess the *likelihood* that any predicted benefit will be realised. A third criterion urges a review of the *quality* of the experiment in relation to its scientific method and the applicability of the proposed techniques. This criterion is possibly the most important as it deals with the methods which are to be used to realise an experiment's aims. Smith and Boyd (1991) suggested that researchers ought to assess their proposed methods in several ways:

- Are the methods relevant in answering a particular scientific question?
- Is it necessary to use animals at all?
- If so, is the species, and number of individuals of that species, appropriate?
- Is it necessary to use procedures of the proposed severity?
- Has the amount of information to be obtained from each animal been maximised, subject to welfare restraints?
- Are the research facilities, scientists and technicians of sufficient quality for the work to be completed successfully?

To this list I would also add:

- Is veterinary advice available, and has the use of anaesthetics and analgesics been given proper consideration?

Anyone closely associated with a particular research project may review their proposed experiment with the above questions in mind and genuinely believe that all have been answered satisfactorily. It is at this point that consultation with colleagues not immediately associated with the proposed research is important. Peer review, properly conducted, provides an effective method of ensuring that most aspects of experimental design are carried out correctly. Colleagues will highlight obvious flaws in reasoning and suggest alternatives. Many research institutions now insist that a thorough peer review process is conducted before any scientist applies for research funding. This necessarily includes in-house seminars for a free exchange of ideas with other scientists and an opportunity for the suggestion of improvements. It also includes mandatory consultation with statisticians to ensure that both the planning and proposed analyses of results are acceptable. Statistical techniques must be used in order to differentiate between the effects of a particular experimental procedure and random variation. A correctly designed experiment will ensure that a researcher can be confident that any results obtained are in response to an experimental manipulation rather than any variability in the system.

An equally important duty of the statistician is to assist in determining how many animals ought to be used for a given procedure. Obviously, it is not appropriate from an ethical standpoint to have too many individuals for each procedure. However, scientists, in their desire to reduce the number of individuals to be used in a proposed experiment, may well weaken their design by having too *few* individuals. This can be as wasteful as having too many, because the experiment will prove statistically inconclusive and have to be repeated to augment the data. A statistician can best determine the appropriate number of animals and treatments to be used to answer a specific question: it is important that all scientists recognise that the contribution of the statistician is indispensable in modern research.

Once an experiment has been designed to the satisfaction of the investigators and their peers (including statisticians), any proposal involving experiments on sentient animals is submitted either to a government representative (e.g. in Britain) or to an Animal Experimentation Ethics Committee (AEEC). In the countries where they have been established, AEECs operate on the basis that human welfare has precedence over the welfare of non-human animals, but that the use of non-humans for scientific purposes is strictly conditional. Generally speaking, AEEC and government guidelines for evaluating proposals make clear that animals should be used only to obtain important information in essential experiments; that all animals used in experiments be treated with respect; and that the welfare of research animals before, during and after experimentation be given careful consideration. With such stipulations in mind, each representative, whether he or she be a British Home Office inspector or an American IACUC member, must balance the potential gains which may accrue beyond an experiment with the inherent costs in terms of distress, poor health or pain of the experimental subjects. It is the responsibility of every inspector or AEEC member to sanction an experiment only when there have been genuine and thorough attempts by the researcher to minimise suffering and when the potential benefits outweigh inherent costs to animals associated with husbandry, housing, experimentation and post-operative conditions.

Refinement alternatives

The third alternative principle is refinement – the modification, to minimise animal suffering, of procedures which must involve sentient animals. Again, it is every researcher's responsibility to answer several questions prior to commencing an experiment. Having first ascertained that the problem is worth solving and that the animal proposed for use is the best model, questions of refinement need to be addressed. Will the experimental subjects be housed adequately? Must the animals be conscious for the procedure? Do I have the appropriate skills to conduct this research humanely? These and other considerations must be given careful thought as part of an 'alternatives' strategy.

A thorough knowledge of the relevant literature is essential. Many professional societies issue guidelines for the use of vertebrates in research, and scientists should make themselves familiar with such publications (see, for example, Anon. 1987, National Health and Medical Research Council 1990b; Association for the Study of Animal Behaviour 1996; American Society of Mammalogists Animal Care and Use Committee 1998). Other refinement techniques include the following:

1. Improved animal husbandry, which reduces the stress of handling and utilises more sympathetic environmental conditions for confining animals.
2. The use of anaesthesia during all surgical procedures and analgesia in postoperative care to alleviate pain.

3. The use of alternative methods of drug and product testing where the severity of endpoints in experiments is reduced.

Improved animal husbandry

Much of the distress which laboratory animals or wild animals held in captivity may endure might not involve actual physical pain. Anxiety, altered physiology due to inadequate exercise or the physiological responses of animals to confinement and handling must all be given due consideration. Environmental conditions within animal houses and laboratories vary enormously. Changes in temperature, humidity, light regime and noise intensity may all contribute to environmental stress. Similarly, the level of animal husbandry may vary during the working week and on weekends, or the standards of diet, bedding, cage cleaning and technical skills of animal house attendants may fluctuate. All of these factors may cause detectable physiological responses to stress which may lead to aberrant results in many experiments. *Stress* is defined here, after Hungarian physiologist Hans Selye (1975, p. 324), as '...the state manifested by a specific syndrome which consists of all non-specifically induced changes within a biological system'.

Anything which produces a state of stress, Selye termed a *stressor*. This definition was later modified to include not only harmful stimuli but also stimuli *perceived* to be harmful (Selye 1976).

The importance of psychological variables in determining the extent of the physiological effects of stressors is well known. Today, stress research emphasises a relationship between physiology and behaviour. For example, an animal exposed to a novel environment is not necessarily in any danger *per se*. Nevertheless, that animal will respond with behavioural changes, increased heart rate and corticosteroid hormone secretion (Moberg 1985). These reactions are indicative of a stress response, even though a new environment does not represent an actual threat to the maintenance of a homeostatic state.

The influence of an individual's perception of a stressor, rather than the stressor itself, is well known. Exposure of laboratory animals to identical physical stressors (e.g. electric shock) with different psychological components (e.g. some individuals given warning buzzers prior to the electric shocks) can result in a different development rate of stomach ulcers – a common pathological symptom of stress. Those individuals which are warned prior to being shocked tend to develop ulcers at an increased rate (Weiss 1972).

Merely having their cages moved by an animal house attendant, something which is done daily as cages and rooms are cleaned, has been found to be a sufficient stressor to alter 19 of 25 measured blood characteristics associated with stress and shock in some strains of laboratory rats (Gärtner *et al.* 1980).

Clearly, anxiety and emotional arousal are factors which can determine the extent of a physiological stress response and must be taken into account in all experiments involving sentient animals.

The adjustment of *wild* mammals to confinement is also relevant to almost all behavioural or physiological studies involving experimentation. Similarly, any long-term studies of the ecology and behaviour of free-living wildlife must take into account any effects of short-term or prolonged physiological responses to capture when the study involves trapping and handling. Prior to experimentation, even highly domesticated species, such as laboratory rats, require extensive periods of acclimation (Grant *et al.* 1971). It is safe to assume that the same must apply to wild mammals in captivity, particularly if a species shows a susceptibility to capture or confinement stress. A great deal of information has been obtained on the behaviour and physiology of wild animals from captive colonies, and the question arises whether such information is pertinent to the species involved or to the conditions in which the animals were held.

Environmental stress can be reduced in animal houses by ensuring:

- appropriate lighting, temperature and humidity control;
- that noise (including ultrasound levels) is kept to an absolute minimum;
- adequate air conditioning to stop the build-up of noxious gases (e.g. ammonia), and to prevent odours from one species (e.g. dogs) from being detected by another species which may be distressed if such odours were detected (e.g. rabbits).

A well-run animal housing facility simply does not have slamming doors, curious and noisy visitors, or unprofessional workers. Ideally, senior staff ought to have veterinary skills and the ability to liaise with research staff to ensure that they are giving due consideration to what happens to their animals before *and* after they have been used in an experiment.

In an important declaration, the British Institute of Medical Ethics Multidisciplinary Working Party on Animal Welfare stated:

> The manner in which laboratory animals are housed and cared for is of utmost importance in determining the overall quality of their lives. Researchers should take particular care for the conditions under which the animals they use are maintained; and housing and husbandry conditions should be taken into account when assessing the overall costs of a particular piece of research. Where possible, more natural or enriched environments should be provided, so that the animals can carry out more of their natural behaviour patterns and fulfil their psychological needs (Smith and Boyd 1991, p. 332).

Carefully controlled husbandry practices, for example providing domestic animals with an opportunity to interact with humans, or keeping wild animals in conditions where interspecific interactions are minimal, will result in healthier animals and the results of any experiments are likely to be more accurate than those of experiments where poorly educated or uncaring researchers have not had the welfare of their animals uppermost in their minds.

The use of anaesthesia and analgesia

The perception of pain   The perception of pain has been the subject of furious debate (see Kuchel, Rose and Burrell 1992). What is pain? We would all agree that, under most circumstances, when we cut ourselves it hurts – but how do you describe what you are feeling to someone else? Pain may be of short or long duration, and can range, subjectively, from mild to severe in intensity. Pain specialists have evaluated pain in humans and emphasise two distinct aspects – stimulus and perception:

> Most authorities agree that pain is a perception, not a physical entity, and that perception of pain depends on a functioning cerebral cortex ... The receptors specifically responsive to noxious stimuli are termed nociceptors. A stimulus must be of a certain strength before a noci-

ceptor will generate nerve impulses in peripheral nerve fibre of which it is a part. This stimulation strength is called the *nociceptive threshold* … The strength at which noxious stimulation is perceived by a human being as pain is referred to as the *pain detection threshold*. The strongest intensity of noxious stimulation that a human being will permit an experimenter to deliver is called the *pain tolerance threshold*. The strength of noxious stimulation necessary to reach the nociceptor threshold is rather constant and varies little among humans and [other] animals. The strength needed to cross the pain detection threshold is slightly more variable, especially among humans experiencing clinical pain. The pain tolerance threshold is the most variable of the three thresholds (Kitchell and Erickson 1983, p. vii).

The important aspect to recognise in this explanation of pain is the interconnection of the two components; *nociception* – the detection and signalling of a noxious stimulus; and the conscious *recognition* of pain derived from that stimulus. Beyond the pain tolerance threshold is *suffering*: '…the affective, behavioural or emotional response to the pain' (Rose and Adams 1989). It is the subjectivity inherent in any perception of a noxious stimulus, the variability in pain tolerance thresholds, and the differing behavioural or emotional responses to pain which make it so difficult to define. Indeed, it may be argued that it is not possible to describe to another the pain one is feeling, or to comprehend another person's misery.

Does the same apply to non-human beings? Do they respond to noxious stimuli differently? As individuals? As species? If so, how do individuals communicate their distress? Are we sufficiently sensitive to detect it?

Philosophers and scientists have wrestled with these questions in an effort to reach consensus on definitions of intraspecific and interspecific pain perception (see Kuchel *et al.* 1992). We have used some non-human species to model pain in humans because the anatomical and chemical pathways by which pain is perceived in these non-humans have been shown to be similar to those in humans (Morton and Griffiths 1985). Is it not logical, then, to reverse the situation and assume that such non-humans perceive pain as we do?

In the absence of objectivity, certain assumptions about pain perception and communication in non-humans have been made. Smith and Boyd (1991) suggested that a non-human being's capacity to experience pain could be tested in two ways. First, does a species have similar anatomical, biochemical and physiological mechanisms '...to those which in a human are known to be correlated with such experiences?' Second, '...does the animal perform in similar ways to humans who are believed to be suffering?' (Smith and Boyd 1991, p. 46). In the absence of a definitive answer to either of these questions, a pragmatic approach can be adopted, based on two assumptions. First, that we accept philosopher Stephen Clark's (1984, p. 42) simple observation that '...pain is painful...' as a working definition of what constitutes pain. Second, although some differences undoubtedly exist between human and non-human beings, conditions which are perceived as painful in humans should be assumed to be perceived as painful in other animals. This assumption formed the basis for the cautious suggestion put forward by Kitchell and Erickson (1983, p. viii):

> When considering pain in animals, analogies must be drawn between human and animal anatomy, physiology and behaviour. Knowledge about pain in animals remains inferential however, and neglect of the probabilistic nature of pain perception in animals leads to anthropomorphism. On the other hand, overemphasis on the uncertainty of our knowledge about pain perception in animals, which leads to a denial that pain perception exists in animals, is logically as well as empirically unfounded. That tacit assumption is that stimuli are noxious and strong enough to give rise to the perception of pain in animals if the stimuli are detected as pain by human beings, if they at least approach or exceed tissue-damaging proportions, and if they produce escape behaviour in animals.

The recognition and alleviation of pain   Pain and distress in animal subjects occur in two main branches of scientific work. The first branch comprises studies which investigate the nature of pain itself. In such procedures, the anatomical, behavioural, chemical and physiological mechanisms associated with pain are monitored, with the ultimate aim being the prevention, reduction or treatment of pain in human and non-human animals (US Congress, Office of Technology Assessment 1986). The testing of analgesic (pain-relieving) drugs may also result in some pain as part of an experimental trial (Morton 1989).

The second branch covers all other kinds of animal experimentation where pain is a completely unintended side-effect which may cloud the results being sought. Despite the difficulties associated with an objective definition of pain (see above), it is important to be able to recognise signs that an animal is in pain. A significant paper published in the British journal *Veterinary Record* in April 1985 detailed ways in which pain, distress and discomfort could be recognised in animals used in experiments (Morton and Griffiths 1985). Researchers were urged to watch for changes in appearance, dietary intake and behaviour, as well as in clinical signs such as altered heart rate, abnormal breathing or muscle twitching. It is important that more than one criterion be used when assessing pain or distress. For example, an animal may appear outwardly to be behaving quite normally but may be losing weight rapidly. The principle to be applied here is – *know your animal*. Learn to recognise symptoms which may indicate that an animal is in pain. These might include (US Congress, Office of Technology Assessment 1986:

- Impaired activity, e.g. an individual may remain immobile in its cage.
- Personality changes such as increased aggression.
- Restlessness, where an animal cannot stay in one position and is constantly getting up and lying down.
- Changes in the rate of intake of food or water.
- Abnormal vocalisation.
- Abnormal posture.
- Self-mutilation.

If it is suspected that an animal is in pain, veterinary advice must be sought, and it is the moral (and, in many countries, the legal) obligation of every researcher to supply pain relief where applicable. This can be done in three ways; *tranquillising, anaesthetising* or administering an *analgesic*.

Tranquillisers have calming effects, reducing anxiety and tension. They lower the level of consciousness but do not offer pain relief. They are particularly suitable in preventing animals struggling while being handled or measured, or for reducing the distress sometimes associated with confinement.

Anaesthetics eliminate the sensation of pain, with varying effects on consciousness. Topical and local anaesthetics do not alter consciousness to the same degree as general anaesthesia. Topical anaesthetics (usually ointments) are used in the treatment of minor injuries; local anaesthetics are used in minor surgery; general anaesthetics render an animal completely unconscious, usually while surgery is conducted. In all cases where an anaesthetic is used, postoperative observation is essential to ensure that anaesthetised areas are not damaged because of a patient's loss of sensation.

Analgesics relieve pain without altering consciousness. They are used most frequently following surgery. In *all* cases where it is likely that pain is perceived, analgesics must be given.

Humane endpoints

Increasing attention is being given to research protocols to determine whether more humane endpoints (the point at which an experiment is deemed to be over) ought to be applied. Pre-lethal, and, ideally, pre-painful endpoints are constantly sought in toxicity trials and drugs testing, where controversial procedures such as the Draize eye instillation test and the LD50 test have been used. Promising alternatives are being developed, including a range of *in-vitro* techniques to replace carcinogenicity and irritancy tests. In one such system, the chorio-allantoic membrane of a chicken embryo (which contains no pain fibres) is used instead of mammals to test products for both skin and eye irritancy (Stephens 1989).

In experiments where tumours are deliberately induced in animals, the severity of an endpoint can be minimised by limiting the size to which the tumour is permitted to grow. Similarly, in certain animal models of disease or in radiation studies, euthanasia ought to be used rather than letting an animal die slowly or painfully.

Alternatives such as those described above point to the future direction of animal experimentation. It is the responsibility of all researchers to modify their techniques to incorporate, where possible, existing alternatives, and to seek novel alternative methods which will continue the reform of animal experimentation.

7   Conclusions

...[the most important issues in debate about animal experimentation are] the assessment of the scientific value of an experiment, of the knowledge or benefit to be gained, and of the suffering (if any) involved, and the question of how to balance these. It is ultimately a moral problem, and a question of responsibility borne both by the scientist and by the rest of society in the characteristically human task of removing ignorance and minimising suffering.

William Paton (1983, p. 104)

THE CONSTRUCTION OF A MODERN RESEARCH
INSTITUTION

In previous chapters, I have emphasised the need for moral consideration in all experiments which involve animals. Despite exhaustive attempts by scientists, theologians, humane philosophers and others to define a single ethical model for animal experimentation, none has proved comprehensive. This does not mean that such an ethic is not attainable – the difficulty lies in individual perceptions of other animals, and to what extent, if any, they ought to be included in our moral sphere. Albert Schweitzer's 'reverence for life' and Peter Singer's 'animal interests' are examples of ethics, derived in different ways, which have prepared the ground for the erection of the modern research institution. Now, and into the future, all such institutions will be staffed by scientists committed to using animals (and sentient animals in particular) in experiments only when it is absolutely necessary. The 'three Rs' of William Russell and Rex Burch (1959) provide solid foundations for construction. Remember, it is by introducing replacement alternatives at every opportunity, reducing the numbers of animals involved in essential experiments, and refining procedures to minimise or eliminate suffering that scientists are best able to justify their research.

This book has been written to help you to form your own opinions about many of the complex issues in animal experimentation. Some readers will be absolutist (wholly for or wholly against animal experiments); others will differ by degrees over the question of which animals ought to be used, and to what extent, for scientific purposes. Many may argue that non-human animals are used of necessity and that this practice ought to continue while suitable alternatives (such as those outlined in Chapter 6) are sought.

In Chapter 2, Claude Bernard was quoted as asking why, in nineteenth-century society, when animals were used for food, transport, sport and entertainment, should they not also be used for scientific research? Contemporary use of non-human animals has not changed greatly since then, so the question he posed in 1865 is as relevant today as it was then.

Modern western society condones intensive animal husbandry practices, such as battery farms for egg production. We condone the use of animals for sport and entertainment at racetracks, rodeos and circuses. We do little in the form of public education campaigns to reduce the numbers of companion animals which are unwanted, abandoned and subsequently euthanased each year. While consumers continue to condone the exhaustive choices of shampoos, perfumes, cleaning products etc. we see on supermarket shelves, so, too, will there be a need for high numbers of animals in safety testing. All of these uses of animals satisfy only present needs. Modern biomedicine offers potential solutions to future needs. It is built on a foundation of animal experimentation and the public favours its continuation.

In science, education and industry, compromise solutions between the abolition of all experimentation and an uncontrolled use of research animals now emphasise the minimisation or elimination of suffering from essential experiments as much as possible. Well-educated scientists now recognise that they have specific obligations to the research animals in their care and strive to ensure that the welfare of their subjects is a high priority.

I introduced this book with a quote by Miriam Rothschild. She recounted how the ethics of zoology were never an overt consideration for her educators. At the end of the twentieth century, the situation had changed drastically for the better. Research animals are now afforded more legislative protection, ethical consideration by scientists and scrutiny by the public than at any other time.

Increasingly, modern life science curricula are taking on board alternative teaching techniques. In some subjects, options are available for students who do not wish to participate in practical classes where experiments using animals are conducted. Animal welfare courses now form essential components of some veterinary training programmes. As the availability of alternatives to invasive procedures becomes more widespread in certain courses (and that availability is advertised beforehand in course outlines), more students may fulfil their interests in life sciences without compromising a chosen ethical stance.

However, students within such courses must recognise their responsibilities. The education offered through the use of animals and animal tissues is not a right – it is a privilege. It is important to recognise this and for students to conduct themselves appropriately in classes where animals are used. To this aim, the Australian and New Zealand Council for the Care of Animals in Research and Teaching (ANZCCART) produced a suite of ethical guidelines which are reproduced at the end of this chapter. If you do not wish to participate in a practical class involving an animal experiment for ethical reasons, do not wait until you get to the class to voice your concerns. By then, an animal may already have been killed for you. See the course co-ordinator well ahead of time. Propose an alternative practical you would like to do. Show the staff your objections are rational and well considered.

Some medical schools conduct special services to remember the people who have donated their bodies to science. Such services aim to instil in students a humility and a respect for the thoughtfulness of others. It would be nice to think the day will come when similar services are held for staff and students to mark the sacrifices made for our benefit by other animals. The humane consideration of the lives of other animals is honourable. Animal rights? Animal interests? Reverence for life? The terminology is unimportant: it is respect for other creatures which is of the utmost importance. Young scientists who carry this respect into their workplace will be instrumental in introducing future alternative methods which continue the reform of animal experimentation.

If you have chosen a career in a biological science, then you carry with you a responsibility to conduct yourself and your research ethically. You have been given a trust by society in general which is not to be taken lightly. Remember, you have chosen an honourable profession – act honourably in all your dealings with other animals and do not lose sight of the sacrifice which we force them to make.

Ethical guidelines for students in laboratory classes involving the use of animals or animal tissues

The following guidelines were produced by ANZCCART with the recommendation that they be displayed prominently in student laboratories and included in laboratory manuals.

Using animals or their tissues in laboratory classes is a privilege which brings with it responsibilities that go well beyond the need to avoid cruelty to the animals.

Outlined below is some advice which will help you to meet these responsibilities and to derive maximum benefit from using animals in laboratory classes. Following this advice will show that you are aware of and accept the responsibilities which accompany the use of animals or their tissues for learning.

THINK ABOUT THE USE OF ANIMALS OR THEIR TISSUES
- Talk about this with other students and staff. Everybody should develop their own opinions about this topic and be prepared to air them, justify them, and modify them. Also, you should feel free to make suggestions which might improve future laboratory classes.

MAKE SURE THAT GOOD USE IS MADE OF THE LEARNING OPPORTUNITY

Be well prepared
- This involves reading background material from lecture notes and references before coming to class, reading the laboratory manual before the class, and being generally prepared to maximise the learning experience.

Think actively during the class
- You should know what underlying principles are being taught in the class and understand the details which illustrate those principles.

This is best achieved by active involvement rather than by merely waiting to be taught.

Participation in the class should be active also

- You should use every opportunity, within the approved scope of the class, to develop manual, observational and recording skills.

Think beyond the immediate scope of the class

- Seeking to link the new knowledge and understanding gained in each class with other parts of the course is a learning device which will help you consolidate your knowledge.

TREAT ANIMALS AND THEIR TISSUES WITH RESPECT AT ALL TIMES AND TAKE PARTICULAR CARE TO TREAT LIVE ANIMALS HUMANELY

- This also means that each person should feel free to seek advice on how to correct a situation when another person does not appear to be meeting this requirement.

References

Adams, R. 1977. *The Plague Dogs*. Harmondsworth: Penguin.

American Medical Association Council on Scientific Affairs 1989. Council report on animals in research. *Journal of the American Medical Association* 261:3602–6.

American Society of Mammalogists Animal Care and Use Committee 1998. Guidelines for the capture, handling, and care of mammals as approved by the American Society of Mammalogists. *Journal of Mammalogy* 79: 1416–31.

Animal Welfare Information Center and Universities Federation for Animal Welfare 1995. *Environmental Enrichment Information Resources for Laboratory Animals: 1965–1995 Birds, Cats, Dogs, Farm Animals, Ferrets, Rabbits and Rodents*. London: UFAW.

Anon. 1987. *Guidelines for Use of Live Amphibians and Reptiles in Field Research*. Gainesville, Florida: Society for the Study of Amphibians and Reptiles.

Anon. 1992. Scientific procedures on living animals, cited in Porter, D.G. Ethical scores for animal experiments. *Nature* 356: 101–2.

Association for the Study of Animal Behaviour 1996. Guidlines for the treatment of animals in behavioural research and teaching. *Animal Behaviour* 51: 241–6.

Australian Council for the Care of Animals in Research and Teaching 1988. *ACCART News* 1(2):6.

Australian Government Senate Select Committee on Animal Welfare 1989. *Animal Experimentation*. Canberra: Australian Government Publishing Service.

Australian and New Zealand Council for the Care of Animals in Research and Teaching 1993a. Scientific procedures on living animals in Great Britain in 1991. *ANZCCART News* 6(1):12.

Australian and New Zealand Council for the Care of Animals in Research and Teaching 1993b. Legal protection for the octopus. *ANZCCART News* 6(4):7.

Bacon, F. 1950. *The Advancement of Learning (1623)*, Kitchin G.W. (ed.) London: Dent.

Balls, M. 1983. Alternatives to animal experimentation. *Alternatives to Laboratory Animals* 11:56–62.

Balls, M. 1990. Recent progress toward reducing the use of animal experimentation in biomedical research. In Garattini, S. and van Bekkum, D.W. (eds.), *The Importance of Animal Experimentation for Safety and Biomedical Research*, pp. 223–35. Dordrecht: Kluwer Academic Publishers.

Battye, J. 1994. Ethics and animal welfare – where do we go from here? In Baker, R.M., Mellor, D.J. and Nicol, A.M. (eds.) *Animal Welfare in the Twenty-First Century: Ethical, Educational and Scientific Challenges*, pp. 3–10. Adelaide: ANZCCART.

Bayne, K.A. and Martin, D.P. 1998. AAALAC International: using performance standards to evaluate an animal care and use program. *Lab Animal* 27 (4):32–5.

Benison, S. 1970. In defense of medical research. *Harvard Medical Bulletin* 44:16–23.

Bentham, J. 1789/1970. An introduction to the principles of morals and legislation. In Burns, J.H. and Hart, H.L.A (eds.), *The Collected Works of Jeremy Bentham*, Vol. 2.1. London: Athlone.

Bernard, C. 1865/1957. *An Introduction to the Study of Experimental Medicine*, trans. Greene, H.C. 1957. New York: Dover.

Birch, C. 1993. *Regaining Compassion for Humanity and Nature*. Kensington: New South Wales University Press.

Bliss, M. 1982. *The Discovery of Insulin*. Chicago: University of Chicago Press.

Boyle, P.R. 1991. *The UFAW Handbook on the Care and Management of Cephalopods in the Laboratory*. London: UFAW.

Brabazon, J. 1976. *Albert Schweitzer: a Biography*. London: Victor Gollancz.

Britt, D. 1984. Ethics, ethical committees and animal experimentation. *Nature* 311:503–6.

Bronowski, J. 1956. *Science and Human Values*, revised edition 1965. New York: Harper and Row.

Callicott, J.B. 1989. *In Defense of the Land Ethic: Essays in Environmental Philosophy*. Albany, NY: State University of New York Press.

Caplan, A. 1989. Cited in *Animal Experimentation, Australian Government Senate Select Committee on Animal Welfare*. Canberra: Australian Government Publishing Service.

Clark, S.R.L. 1984. *The Moral Status of Animals*. Oxford: Oxford University Press.

Cottingham, J. 1978. A brute to the brutes?: Descartes' treatment of animals. *Philosophy* 53:551–9.

Cranefield, P.F. 1974. *The Way In and the Way Out: François Magendie, Charles Bell, and the Roots of the Spinal Nerves*. New York: Futura.

Darwin, C. 1859/1964. *On the Origin of Species by Natural Selection*. Facsimile of the first edition reprinted by Harvard University Press, Cambridge, MA.

Darwin, C. 1871/1981. *The Descent of Man, and Selection in Relation to Sex*. Facsimile of the first edition reprinted by Princeton University Press, Princeton, NJ.

Darwin, C. 1881/1985. *The Formation of Vegetable Mould, through the Action of Worms*. Facsimile of the first edition reprinted by the University of Chicago Press, Chicago.

Denton, D. 1993. *The Pinnacle of Life: Consciousness and Self-Awareness in Humans and Animals*. Sydney: Allen and Unwin.

Di Marco, P.N., Howell, J.McC. and Dorling, P.R. 1984. Bovine glycogenosis type II. Biochemical and morphological characteristics of skeletal muscle in culture. *Neuropathology and Applied Neurobiology* 10:379–95.

Descartes, R. 1637/1984. *Discours de la Méthode*, trans. Curtis, D. London: Grant and Cutler.

Draize, J.H., Woodward, G. and Calvery, H.O. 1944. Methods for the study of irritation and toxicity of substances applied to the skin and mucous membranes. *Journal of Pharmacology and Experimental Therapy* 82:377.

Duckworth, W.L.H., Lyons, M.C. and Towers, B. (eds.) 1962. *Galen, On Anatomical Procedures: the Later Books*. Cambridge: Cambridge University Press.

Eisemann, C.H., Jorgensen, W.K., Merritt, D. J., Rice, M.J., Cribb, B.W., Webb, P.D. and Zalucki, M.P. 1984. Do insects feel pain? – A biological view. *Experientia* 40:164–7.

Enders, J.F., Weller, T.H. and Robbins, F.C. 1949. Cultivation of the Lansing strain of poliomyelitis virus in cultures of various human embryonic tissue. *Science* 109:85–7.

Fisher, J.A. 1987. Taking sympathy seriously: a defense of our moral psychology toward animals. *Environmental Ethics* 9:197–215.

Flemming, A. H. 1984. *Ethical Considerations, 1984*, cited in US Congress, Office of Technology Assessment, 1986, *Alternatives to Animal Use in Research, Testing, and Education*, p. 74. New York: Marcel Dekker.

Flexner, S. and Lewis, P.A. 1909. The transmission of acute poliomyelitis to monkeys. *Journal of the American Medical Association* 53:1639.

FRAME Toxicity Committee 1991. Animals and alternatives in toxicology: present status and future prospects. *Alternatives to Laboratory Animals* 19: 116–38.

French, R.D. 1975. *Antivivisection and Medical Science in Victorian Society*. Princeton, NJ: Princeton University Press.

French, R.D. 1978. Animal experimentation: historical aspects. In Reich, W.T. (ed.), *Encyclopedia of Bioethics*, Vol. 1, pp. 75–9. New York: Free Press.

Galen, 1956. *On Anatomical Procedures*, trans. Singer, C. Oxford: Oxford University Press.

Galvin, S.L. and Herzog, H.A. Jr 1998. Attitudes and dispositional optimism of animal rights demonstrators. *Society and Animals* 6:1–11.

Gärtner, K., Büttner, D., Döhler, K., Friedel, R., Lindena, J. and Trautschold, I. 1980. Stress response of rats to handling and experimental procedures. *Laboratory Animals* 14:267–74.

Grant, L., Hopkinson, P., Jennings, G. and Jenner, F.A. 1971. Period of adjustment of rats used for experimental studies. *Nature* 232:135.

Gruen, L. 1991. Animals. In Singer, P. (ed.), *A Companion to Ethics*, pp. 343–53. Oxford: Blackwell Reference.

Hamm, T.E., Dell, R.B. and Van Sluyters, R.C. 1995. Laboratory animal care policies and regulations: United States. *ILAR Journal* 37:75–8.

Hampson, J. 1989. Legislation and the changing consensus. In Langley, G. (ed.), *Animal Experimentation: the Consensus Changes*, pp. 219–51. London: MacMillan Press.

Hart, L.A. 1998. Responsible animal care and use: moving toward a less-troubled middle ground. In Hart, L.A. (ed.), *Responsible Conduct with Animals in Research*, pp. 1–17. New York: Oxford University Press.

Harvey, W. 1628/1978. Exercitatio anatomica de motu cordis et sanguinis in animalibus: being a facsimile of the 1628 Francofurti edition, together with the Keynes English translation of 1928. Birmingham, AL: Classics of Medicine Library.

Hills, A.M. 1994. Motives underlying attitudes toward the use of animals in teaching and research. *ANZCCART News* 7(3):3–4.

Howell, J.McC., Dorling, P.R. and Cook, R.D. 1983. Generalized glycogenosis type II. *Comparative Pathology Bulletin*, 15:2–4.

Hume, C.W. 1962. *Man and Beast*. London: UFAW.

Humphrey, N.K. 1983. *Consciousness Regained: Chapters in the Development of Mind*. Oxford: Oxford University Press.

Infield, L. 1963. *Immanuel Kant: Lectures on Ethics*. New York: Harper and Row.

Ingle, R. 1995. *The UFAW Handbook on the Care and Management of Decapod Crustaceans in Captivity*. London: UFAW.

Institute of Laboratory Animal Resources 1995. Laboratory animal care policies and regulations. *ILAR Journal* 37:55–78.

Kitchell, R.L. and Erickson, H.H. 1983. Introduction. In Kitchell, R.L. and Erickson, H.H. (eds.), *Animal Pain: Perception and Alleviation*, p.vii. Bethesda: American Physiological Society.

Kuchel. T. R., Rose, M. and Burrell, J. (eds.) 1992. *Animal Pain: Ethical and Scientific Perspectives*. Adelaide: ACCART.

Langley, G. 1989. Plea for a sensitive science. In Langley, G. (ed.), *Animal Experimentation: the Consensus Changes*, pp. 193–218. Oxford: MacMillan Press.

Lederer, S.E. 1987. The controversy over animal experimentation in America, 1880–1914. In Rupke, N.A. (ed.), *Vivisection in Historical Perspective*, pp. 236–58. London: Croom Helm.

Leopold, A. 1949. *A Sand County Almanac*. Oxford: Oxford University Press.

Linzey, A. 1989. Reverence, responsibility and rights. In Paterson, D. and Palmer M. (eds.), *The Status of Animals: Ethics, Education and Welfare*, pp. 20–50. Oxford: CABI.

Maehle, A-H. and Tröhler, U. 1987. Animal experimentation from antiquity to the end of the eighteenth century: attitudes and arguments. In Rupke, N.A. (ed.), *Vivisection in Historical Perspective*, pp. 14–47. London: Croom Helm.

Manning, H. 1887/1934. *Cardinal Manning, Archbishop of Westminster on Vivisection*. London: Victoria Street Society for the Protection of Animals from Vivisection. Republished Melbourne.

Moberg, G. 1985. Biological response to stress: key to assessment of animal well-being? In Moberg, G. (ed.), *Animal Stress*, pp. 27–49. Bethesda: American Physiological Society.

Morton, D.B. 1989. The scientist's responsibility for refinement: a guide to better animal welfare and better science. In Langley, G. (ed.), *Animal Experimentation: the Consensus Changes.* pp. 169–92. Oxford: MacMillan Press.

Morton, D.B. and Griffiths, P.H.M. 1985. Guidelines on the recognition of pain, distress and discomfort in experimental animals and an hypothesis for assessment. *Veterinary Record* 116: 431–6.

Mukerjee, M. 1997. Trends in animal research. *Scientific American* 276:70–7.

Nash, R.F. 1990. *The Rights of Nature*. Sydney: Primavera Press.

National Health and Medical Research Council 1990a. *Strategies for Minimising the Numbers of Animals used in Research Projects*. Canberra: Australian Government Publishing Service.

National Health and Medical Research Council 1990b. *A Guide to the Use of Australian Native Mammals in Biomedical Research*. Canberra: Australian Government Publishing Service.

National Health and Medical Research Council 1997. *Australian Code of Practice for the Care and Use of Animals for Scientific Purposes*, sixth edition. Canberra: Australian Government Publishing Service.

National Research Council 1985. *Models for Biomedical Research: a New Perspective*. Washington DC: National Academy Press.

National Research Council 1988. *Use of Laboratory Animals in Biomedical and Behavioral Research*. Washington DC: National Academy Press.

National Research Council 1996. *Guide for the Care and Use of Laboratory Animals*. Washington DC: US Department of Health and Human Services.

Orlans, F.B. 1993. *In the Name of Science: Issues in Responsible Animal Experimentation*. New York: Oxford University Press.

Paton, W.D.M. 1983. Vivisection, morals, medicine: commentary from a vivisecting professor of pharmacology. *Journal of Medical Ethics* 9:102–4.

Paton, W.D.M. 1993. *Man and Mouse: Animals in Medical Research*, second edition. Oxford: Oxford University Press.

Paver, M. 1998. Legislation and regulation: a view from the UK. In Holland, A. and Johnson, A. (eds.), *Animal Biotechnology and Ethics*, pp. 276–87. London: Chapman and Hall.

Phillips, M.T. and Sechzer, J.A. 1989. *Animal Research and Ethical Conflict: an Analysis of the Scientific Literature 1966–1986*. New York: Springer-Verlag.

Poling, A., Schlinger, H., Starin, S. and Blakely, E. 1990. *Psychology: a Behavioral Overview*. New York: Plenum Press.

Poole, T. (ed.) 1999a. UFAW Handbook on the Care and Management of Laboratory Animals, Vol. 1, *Terrestrial Vertebrates*. Oxford: Blackwell Science.

Poole, T. (ed.) 1999b. UFAW Handbook on the Care and Management of Laboratory Animals, Vol. 2, *Amphibious and Aquatic Vertebrates and Advanced Invertebrates*. Oxford: Blackwell Science.

Porter, D.G. 1992. Ethical scores for animal experiments. *Nature* 356:101–2.

Regan, T. 1981. Animal rights and animal experimentation. In Basson, M.D. (ed.), *Rights and Responsibilities in Modern Medicine*, pp. 69–83. New York: Alan R. Liss.

Regan, T. 1982. *All That Dwell Therein: Animal Rights and Environmental Ethics.* Berkeley: University of California Press.

Regan, T. 1983. *The Case for Animal Rights.* Berkeley: University of California Press.

Regan, T. 1985. The case for animal rights. In Singer, P. (ed.), *In Defense of Animals,* pp. 13–26. Oxford: Basil Blackwell.

Regan, T. 1990. The struggle for animal rights. In Clarke, P.A.B. and Linzey, A. (eds.), *Political Theory and Animal Rights,* pp. 176–86. London: Pluto Press.

Regan, T. and Singer, P. (eds.) 1976. *Animal Rights and Human Obligations.* Englewood Cliffs, NJ: Prentice-Hall.

Remfry, J. 1987. Ethical aspects of animal experimentation. In Tuffrey, A.A. (ed.), *Laboratory Animals: an Introduction for New Experimenters,* pp. 5–19. Chichester: John Wiley and Sons.

Rodd, R. 1990. *Biology, Ethics and Animals.* Oxford: Clarendon Press.

Rollin, B.E. 1981. *Animal Rights and Human Morality.* New York: Prometheus.

Rollin, B.E. 1995. Laws relevant to animal research in the United States. In Tuffery, A.A. (ed.), *Laboratory Animals – an Introduction for Experimenters,* second edition, pp. 67–86. Chichester: John Wiley and Sons.

Rolston, H. 1988. *Environmental Ethics: Duties to and Values in the Natural World.* Philadelphia: Temple University Press.

Rose, M. and Adams, D. 1989. Evidence for pain and suffering in other animals. In Langley G. (ed.), *Animal Experimentation: the Consensus Changes,* pp. 42–71. Oxford: MacMillan Press.

Rosenfield, L.C. 1940. *From Beast-Machine to Man-Machine.* Oxford: Oxford University Press.

Rothschild, M. 1986. *Animals and Man. The Romanes Lecture for 1984–85.* Oxford: Clarendon Press.

Rowan, A.N. 1984. *Of Mice, Models and Men: a Critical Evaluation of Animal Research.* Albany, NY: State University of New York Press.

Rowan, A.N. and Rollin, B.E. 1983. Animal research – for and against: a philosophical, social, and historical perspective. *Perspectives in Biology and Medicine* 27: 1–17.

Rupke, N.A. 1987. Introduction. In Rupke, N.A. (ed.), *Vivisection in Historical Perspective,* pp. 1–13. London: Croom Helm.

Russell, W.M.S. and Burch, R.L. 1959. *The Principles of Humane Experimental Technique.* London: Methuen.

Ryder, R.D. 1975. *Victims of Science: the Use of Animals in Research.* London: Davis-Poynter.

Ryder, R.D. 1989. *Animal Revolution: Changing Attitudes Towards Speciesism.* Oxford: Basil Blackwell.

Sagan, C. and Druyan, A. 1992. *Shadows of Forgotten Ancestors: a Search for Who We Are.* Sydney: Random House.

Schweitzer, A. 1936. *Indian Thought and its Development.* London: Adam and Charles Black.

Schweitzer, A. 1955. *Civilization and Ethics,* third edition. London: Adam and Charles Black.

Schweitzer, A. 1966. *My Life and Thought: an Autobiography.* London: Unwin Books.

Selye, H. 1975. *The Stress of Life,* second edition. New York: McGraw-Hill.

Selye, H. 1976. *Stress in Health and Disease.* Boston: Butterworths.

Seyfarth, R.M., Cheney, D.L. and Marler, P. 1980. Monkey responses to three different alarm calls: evidence for predator classification and semantic communication. *Science* 210:801–3.

Shakespeare, W. 1982. Cymbeline, Scene Five. In *The Complete Works of William Shakespeare,* pp. 965–97. Cambridge: Cambridge University Press.

Shaw, G.B. 1912. *The Uselessness of the Vivisection Inspector.* London: British Union for the Abolition of Vivisection.

Shugg, W. 1968a. Humanitarian attitudes in the early animal experiments of the Royal Society. *Annals of Science* 24:227–38.

Shugg, W. 1968b. The Cartesian beast-machine in English literature (1663–1750). *Journal of the History of Ideas* 29: 279–92.

Singer, C.J. 1957. *A Short History of Anatomy from the Greeks to Harvey*, second edition. New York: Dover Publications.

Singer, P. 1975. *Animal Liberation*. New York: Avon Books.

Singer, P. 1978. Animal experimentation: philosophical perspectives. In Reich, W.T. (ed.), *Encyclopedia of Bioethics*, Vol. 1, pp. 79–83. New York: Free Press.

Singer, P. 1979. *Practical Ethics*. Cambridge: Cambridge University Press.

Singer, P. 1990. *Animal Liberation*, second edition. London: Jonathan Cape.

Singer, P. 1993. *Practical Ethics*, second edition. Cambridge: Cambridge University Press.

Smith, J.A. and Boyd, K.M. (eds.) 1991. *Lives in the Balance: the Ethics of Using Animals in Biomedical Research*. Oxford: Oxford University Press.

Smyth, D.H. 1978. *Alternatives to Animal Experiments*. London: Scolar Press.

Stephens, M.L. 1986. *Maternal Deprivation Experiments in Psychology: a Critique of Animal Models*. Pennsylvania: The American Anti-Vivisection Society.

Stephens, M.L. 1989. Replacing animal experiments. In Langley, G. (ed.), *Animal Experimentation: the Consensus Changes*, pp. 144–68. Oxford: MacMillan Press.

Stevens, C. 1990. Laboratory animal welfare. In Leavett, E.S. (ed.), *Animals and their Legal Rights*, pp. 66–105. Washington DC: Animal Welfare Institute.

Stone, M. 1989. Cited in *Animal Experimentation, Australian Government Senate Select Committee on Animal Welfare*. Canberra: Australian Government Publishing Service.

Straughan, D.W. and Balls, M. 1998. Controls on the care and use of experimental animals. In Holland, A. and Johnson, A. (eds.), *Animal Biotechnology and Ethics*, pp. 303–21. London: Chapman and Hall.

Townsend, P. and Morton, D.B. 1995. Laboratory animal care policies and regulations: United Kingdom. *ILAR Journal* 37:68–74.

Turner, J. 1980. *The Nature of the Beast: Animals, Pain and Humanity in the Victorian Mind*. Baltimore: Johns Hopkins University Press.

UK Home Office 1999. *Report of the Animal Procedures Committee for 1998*. London: The Stationery Office.

Universities Federation for Animal Welfare and Fund for the Replacement of Animals in Medical Experiments 1998. *Selection and Use of Replacement Methods in Animal Experimentation*. London: UFAW.

US Congress, Office of Technology Assessment 1986. *Alternatives to Animal Use in Research, Testing, and Education*. Washington DC: US Government Printing Office.

Voltaire, 1764/1962. *Philosophical Dictionary*, trans. Gay, P. New York: Basic Books, pp. 112–13.

Wade, N. 1978. New vaccine may bring man and chimpanzee into tragic conflict. *Science* 200: 1027–30.

Wall, P.D. 1992. Humane treatment of animals does not mean treating animals as humans. In Kuchel, T. R., Rose, M. and Burrell, J. (eds.), *Animal Pain: Ethical and Scientific Perspectives*, pp. 1–12. Adelaide: ACCART.

Weiss, J.M. 1972. Psychological factors in stress and disease. *Scientific American* 226:104–13.

Wilkins, D. 1997. *Animal Welfare in Europe: European Legislation and Concerns*. The Hague: Kluwer Law International.

Wong, J. 1995. Laboratory animal care policies and regulations: Canada. *ILAR Journal* 37: 57–9.

Appendix: recommended further reading

American Veterinary Association 1973. *Principles of Veterinary Medical Ethics*. Chicago: American Veterinary Association.

Baird, R.M. and Rosenbaum, S.E. (eds.) 1991. *Animal Experimentation: the Moral Issues*. New York: Prometheus.

Balls, M., Riddell, R.J. and Worden, A.N. (eds.) 1983. *Animals and Alternatives in Toxicity Testing*. London: Academic Press.

Biological Council 1984. *Guidelines on the Use of Living Animals in Scientific Investigations*. London: Biological Council.

Boakes, R. 1984. *From Darwinism to Behaviourism: Psychology and the Minds of Animals*. Cambridge: Cambridge University Press.

Clark, S.R.L. 1982. *The Nature of the Beast: Are Animals Moral?* Oxford: Oxford University Press.

Darwin, C. 1872/1969. *The Expression of the Emotions in Man and Animals*. New York: Greenwood Press.

Dawkins, M.S. 1980. *Animal Suffering: the Science of Animal Welfare*. London: Chapman and Hall.

Dodds, W.J. and Orlans, F.B. (eds.) 1982. *Scientific Perspectives on Animal Welfare*. New York: Academic Press.

Fox, M.A. 1986. *The Case for Animal Experimentation: an Evolutionary and Ethical Perspective*. Berkeley: University of California Press.

Fox, M.W. 1986. *Laboratory Animal Husbandry: Ethology, Welfare and Experimental Variables*. Albany, NY: State University of New York Press.

Fox, M.W. and Mickley, L.D. (eds.) 1987. *Advances in Animal Welfare Science, 1986/1987*. The Hague: Martinus Nijhoff.

Frey, R.G. 1980. *Interests and Rights: the Case against Animals*. Oxford: Oxford University Press.

Frey, R.G. 1983. *Rights, Killing and Suffering: Moral Vegetarianism and Applied Ethics*. Oxford: Basil Blackwell.

Gibson, T.E. (ed.), 1981. *The Detection and Relief of Pain in Animals*. London: British Veterinary Association Animal Welfare Foundation.

Griffin, D. 1981. *The Question of Animal Awareness*. Los Altos, CA: William Kaufman.

Griffin, D. 1984. *Animal Thinking*. Cambridge, MA: Harvard University Press.

Leahy, M. 1991. *Against Liberation: Putting Animals in Perspective*. London: Routledge.

Magel, C. H. 1989. *Keyguide to Information Sources in Animal Rights*. London: Mansell.

Midgley, M. 1983. *Animals and Why They Matter*. Athens GA: University of Georgia Press.

National Institute of Health 1985. *Guide for the Care and Use of Laboratory Animals*. Bethesda: National Institute of Health.

Pratt, D. 1980. *Alternatives to Pain in Experiments on Animals*, New York: Argus Archives.

Rachels, J. 1990. *Created from Animals: the Moral Implications of Darwinism*. Oxford: Oxford University Press.

Reinhardt, C.A. (ed.) 1994. *Alternatives to Animal Testing: New Ways in the Biomedical Sciences, Trends and Progress*. Weinheim, Germany: Wiley–VCH.

Ridley, M. (ed.) 1987. *The Essential Darwin*. London: Unwin.

Rollin, B.E. 1989. *The Unheeded Cry: Animal Consciousness, Animal Pain and Science*. Oxford: Oxford University Press.

Sapontzis, S.F. 1987. *Morals, Reason, and Animals*. Philadelphia: Temple University Press.

Schweitzer, A. 1966. *The Teaching of Reverence for Life*, trans. Winston, R. and Winston, C. London: Peter Owen.

Sharpe, R. 1988. *The Cruel Deception: the Use of Animals in Medical Research*. Wellingborough, Northants: Thorsons Publishing Group.

Sperlinger, D. (ed.) 1981. *Animals in Research: New Perspectives in Animal Experimentation*. Chichester: John Wiley and Sons.

Stephens, M.L. 1986. *Alternatives to Current Uses of Animals in Research, Safety Testing, and Education*. Washington, DC: The Humane Society, USA.

Stratmann, G.C., Stratmann, C.J. and Paxton, C. 1987. *Animal Experiments and Their Alternatives*. Braunton, Devon: Merlin Books.

Thomas, K. 1983. *Man and the Natural World*. London: Allen Lane.

Webster, J. 1995. *Animal Welfare: a Cool Eye towards Eden*. Melbourne: Blackwell.

Index